Mental Math Workout

Michael L. Lobosco

Sterling Publishing Co., Inc. New York

A Sterling/Tamos Book

A Sterling/Tamos Book
© 1998 Michael L. Lobosco

Sterling Publishing Co., Inc.
387 Park Avenue South,
New York, NY 10016–8810

TAMOS Books Inc.
300 Wales Avenue, Winnipeg, Manitoba, Canada R2M 2S9

10   9   8   7   6   5   4   3   2   1

Distributed in Canada by Sterling Publishing Co., Inc.
c/o Canadian Manda Group, One Atlantic Avenue, Suite 105
Toronto, Ontario, Canada M6K 3E7
Distributed in Great Britain and Europe by Cassell PLC,
Wellington House, 125 Strand, London WC2R 0BB, England
Distributed in Australia by Capricorn Link (Australia) Pty Ltd.
P.O. Box 6651, Baulkham Hills, Business Centre,
NSW 2153, Australia

Design A. O. Osen
Photography Jerry Grajewski, Custom Images

Printed in China

Canadian Cataloging-in-Publication Data
Lobosco, Michael L. (Michael Louis), 1918–
        Mental math workout
        "A Sterling/Tamos book."
        Includes index.
        ISBN 1-895569-27-3
        1. Mathematical recreations. I. Title.
QA95.L623 1998   793.7'4   C97–920123–3

Library of Congress Cataloging-in-Publication Data
Lobosco, Michael L.
        Mental math workout / Michael L. Lobosco.
            p.   cm.
        "A Sterling/Tamos book."
        Includes index.
        ISBN 1-895569-27-3
        1. Mathematics--Study and teaching. 2. Creative activities
and seat work.   I. Title.
QA11.L738   1998
510'.78--dc21   97-44396
                                                       CIP

ISBN 1-895569-27-3

Contents

POSSIBILITIES

The more faith you have,

The more you believe,

The more goals you set,

The more you'll achieve …

So reach for the stars,

Pick a mountain to climb,

Dare to think big,

And give yourself time …

And, remember no matter

How futile things seem,

With faith, there is no

Impossible dream!

from
Reflections of Love
Alice Joyce Davidson

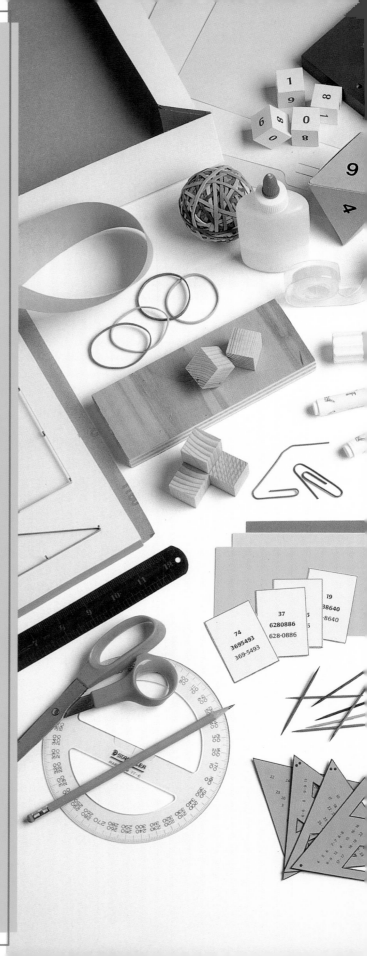

Introduction

Imagine making fifteen different designs by simply flexing a magical hexagon, or adding in your head numbers like 642, 780, 855, and 773 faster than a calculator, or reciting from memory any one of 25 telephone numbers. It's possible by learning a simple math idea! Would you like these math miracles to be yours? All you need is a little practice, and help from this book!

The aim of MENTAL MATH WORKOUT is to give you some unusual math ideas and a wealth of hands-on, do-it-yourself activities so that you can make the math ideas work. The activities are fun to do and you will find them surprisingly beautiful, mysteriously magical, and richly satisfying. Each of the projects will stretch your mind, tickle your math funny bone, and provide hours of pleasure for you alone or with a friend matching wits in a game of strategy.

Let me quickly assure you that this is not another collection of puzzles and problems like a cookbook of basic recipes. These "think exercises," mostly originals or newer adaptations of oldies, are tested action projects—things to make and experiments to do. They take math out of the paper-and-pencil class and make it something more than merely manipulating numbers in a workbook.

This book uses inexpensive supplies. Where other hands-on math projects, catalogs, and books use more costly school supplies such as plastic shapes and cubes, gameboards, checkers, dice, markers, and more, the projects in this book require small inexpensive items such as toothpicks, rubber bands, staples, tape, dowels, and sandpaper.

You can also use recycled materials. Cardboard boxes and cartons from stores, wooden blocks and plywood scraps from lumber yards and construction sites, discarded manila folders from banks and offices are the basic materials needed for the projects. All of these can be obtained at minimum cost for one person or for group participation in a classroom.

This book helps you learn by doing. Once the projects have been completed and the constructions made, you can transfer the skills you have learned to other areas. Construction details do not require skilled carpentry—only measuring, drawing, cutting, and assembling. Anyone can do it. It's a fun, do-it-yourself experience.

Symmetry and Beauty in Math

Hexagon Color Mixer and Design Maker

The hexagon shape that flexes (hexaflexagon) is the most popular geometric paper model. It can produce many colors and designs, almost magically. By flexing from a group of many colored concentric circles, the hexaflexagon can be transformed to a colored triangle design, then to a star, a cube design, or any other patterns you choose. Not only can six different colors be produced, but also fifteen symmetrical patterns can be created using different line designs (see diagram).

Materials Needed
Paper strip 3 in x 42 in (7.6 cm x 106.7 cm)
Protractor
Scissors
Paste or glue
6 colored pencils

Construction

1 Measure a 60 degree angle at one end of the paper strip, draw a line, and cut, as shown.

2 Fold the angle edge so that it meets the upper edge of the strip to form an equilateral triangle. Then fold to meet the lower edge of the strip, as shown. Continue folding until you have 19 triangles.

3 Number the top and under surfaces, as shown.

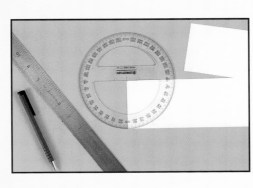

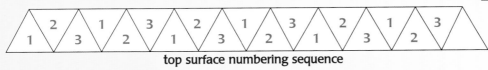

top surface numbering sequence

under surface numbering sequence

4 To form the hexaflexagon, hold the strip so that the under surface is visible. Start folding from the left so that the triangle numbered 4 folds onto the other triangle numbered 4. Continue folding like numbers together, 5 on 5, 6 on 6, 4 on 4, and so on. When completed, the strip will have only 1s, 2s, and 3s visible.

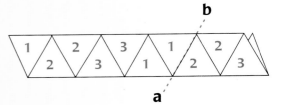

5 Using a ruler, make a dotted line, **ab**, as shown.

6 Fold under on dotted line **ab**, then turn over so that the strip looks like the diagram shown.

7 Then make dotted line **cd**, and fold under along this line (see diagram). Two more triangles numbered 2 will appear and will complete the hexaflexagon.

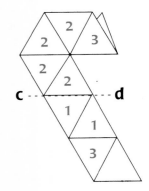

8 Paste the unnumbered triangle to the other blank triangle.

9 The top surface of the hexaflexagon will have six triangles all numbered 1. These penciled numbers can now be erased and the triangles colored and/or designed, as shown on page 8, or in colors and patterns of your choice.

How to Mix the Colors

As the hexaflexagon is folded and reopened, different designs and colors are magically produced. This color mixer makes colors appear and vanish in an amusing and logical order.

1 Hold the hexagon by two opposite corners with one color (or pattern) facing away from you, and another color (or pattern) facing toward you, as shown.

2 Place your left thumb on the **fold line** between two triangular sections, with the rest of the fingers of your left hand on the back side, away from you.

3 Allow your right thumb and forefinger to straddle the **fold line** between two sections, as shown. Your right middle finger is underneath the thumb and forefinger.

4 Pinch these sections around your middle right finger, and at the same time push the two sections at the fold, where the left thumb is, inward to the center, so that the hexagon now collapses into a three-pointed star, as shown.

5 Note the position of the left thumb in the photograph. It can now grasp the corners of two sections in the center of the star and open up the figure to form a new hexagon as you relax the grip of your right hand and allow all sections to open up.

Sample patterns showing change when flexed

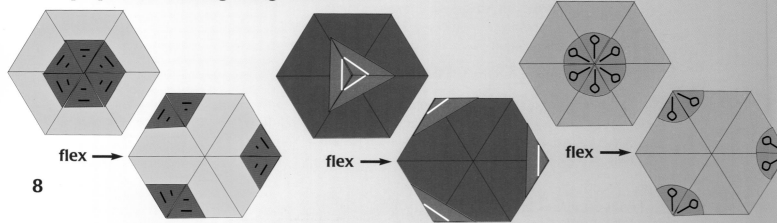

flex →

flex →

flex →

Curved Designs from Straight Lines

Can you make artistic curves from straight lines? Try the exercises on the following pages, then surprise yourself by producing a beautifully curved masterpiece with only a ruler and a colored pen or pencil.

All of these curving designs are created from straight lines drawn within certain angles. After creating your own colorful curves using models 1, 2, 3, and 4, you will feel like a math-artist. You can then enlarge your favorite work on a larger sheet of paper using the same angles and adding more points on the lines.

Materials Needed

4 sheets of standard paper
Ruler
Pencil
Colored pens or pencils

Construction

1   Using one sheet of standard paper, ruler, and pencil, draw model 1 starting at the lower left corner, as shown on page 10 (enlarge models to desired size).

2   Mark off points along each line every ¼ in (0.6 cm).

3   Number points on left line 1 to 31 starting at the top and moving downward. *Do not number the point where the two lines meet.*

4   Number points on the right line 1 to 31 starting at the bottom and moving upward.

5   Connect point to point joining same numbers. For example, 1 to 1, 2 to 2, 3 to 3, etc.

6   Using another sheet of paper, draw model 2, as shown on page 10.

7   Connect 1 to 1, 2 to 2, 3 to 3, etc., along each side of Y figure. Connect 1 to 12, 2 to 11, 3 to 10, etc. in the V portion of the Y shape, as indicated.

8   Using another sheet of paper, draw model 3, as shown on page 11.

9   Connect 1 to 1, 2 to 2, 3 to 3, etc., along each side of the figure.

10   Using another sheet of paper, draw model 4, as shown on page 11.

11   Connect 1 to 1, 2 to 2, 3 to 3, etc., along each triangle space.

Optional   **To create string art from your design, transfer your paper design to a fabric-covered wallboard or plywood. Wherever the points are located on paper, place a pin or small nail. Use colored string, nylon, or yarn to make the lines connecting the points.**

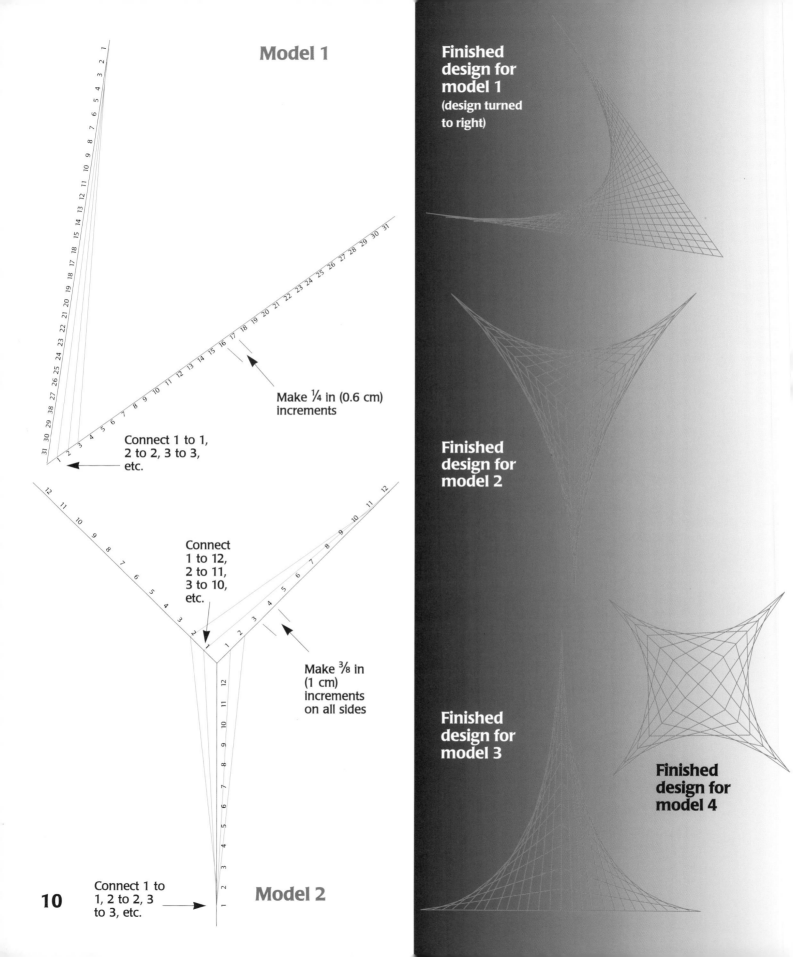

Model 1

Make ¼ in (0.6 cm) increments

Connect 1 to 1, 2 to 2, 3 to 3, etc.

Connect
1 to 12,
2 to 11,
3 to 10,
etc.

Make ⅜ in
(1 cm)
increments
on all sides

Connect 1 to
1, 2 to 2, 3
to 3, etc.

Model 2

Finished
design for
model 1
(design turned
to right)

Finished
design for
model 2

Finished
design for
model 3

Finished
design for
model 4

Model 3

Connect 1 to 1,
2 to 2, 3 to 3,
etc. →

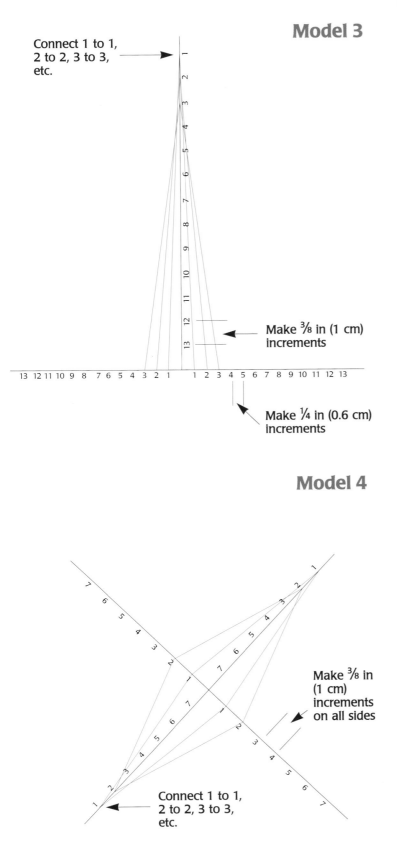

Make ³⁄₈ in (1 cm)
increments

13 12 11 10 9 8 7 6 5 4 3 2 1   1 2 3 4 5 6 7 8 9 10 11 12 13

Make ¼ in (0.6 cm)
increments

Model 4

Make ³⁄₈ in
(1 cm)
increments
on all sides

Connect 1 to 1,
2 to 2, 3 to 3,
etc.

**Can you discover the
models used to make the
above design?**

11

Line Designs Within a Circle

Materials Needed

Sheets of paper
Compass
Ruler
Colored pencils

Construction

1 Using the compass, make three circles, each 2 in (5.1 cm) in diameter, as shown below.

2 In one circle mark six points on the circumference using compass opened to original circle radius (1 in or 2.5 cm). Number these points 1, 2, 3, 4, 5, and 6. Draw lines connecting every other point: 1 to 3, 3 to 5, and 5 to 1, to form a triangle.

3 In another circle mark six points in exactly the same manner as in step 2. Number points 1, 2, 3, 4, 5, and 6. Draw lines connecting these points in succession, to form a hexagon.

4 In the remaining circle, draw a straight dotted line through the center of the circle. Label points where dotted line intersects the circumference, **A** and **B**. Draw another dotted line through center of circle at a right angle to **AB**. Label points **C** and **D**, as shown. Connect points in succession to form a square.

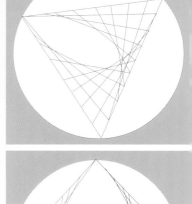

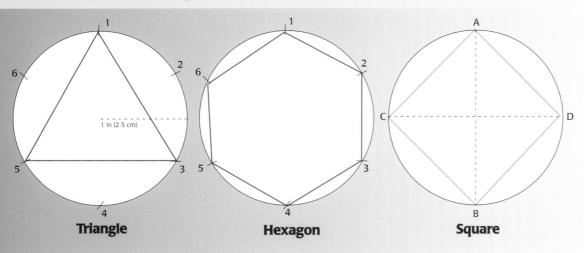

Triangle   **Hexagon**   **Square**

5 Using colored pencils and a ruler, draw curved designs from straight lines (page 9) within these shapes to create beautiful art designs.

These five designs were created from three basic circle constructions. With colored pencils and ingenuity and experimentation many more artistic drawings can be created.

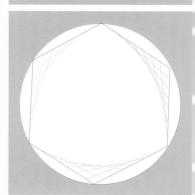

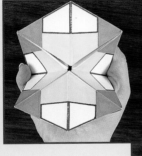

Inverting Pyramid Ring

This paper model, when constructed, opens up in your hands like a flower, four times, and creates different composite pictures each time. The unusual ring has eight connected pyramids and is made from a strip of heavy paper. Flex the ring for friends and amaze them with the magical array of pictures or designs you can bring forth.

Materials Needed

Strip of heavy paper 24 in x 6 in
(61 cm x 15.2 cm)
Protractor
Ruler
Colored pens or markers
Glue

13

Construction

1 Draw line **XY** lengthwise along the center of the paper strip. Mark the line in sections 2⅜ in (6 cm) long. (See diagram.) With a protractor draw dotted lines, as shown, making a 60 degree angle at each 2⅜ in (6 cm) mark.

2 Do the same with solid lines in the other direction at a 60 degree angle.

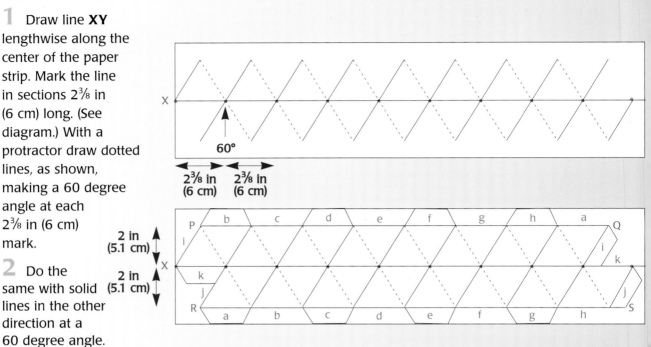

3 Complete the triangles by drawing horizontal lines, **PQ** and **RS**, 2 in (5.1 cm) above and below the center line **XY**.

4 Draw the tabs, as shown, and cut out the network including all tabs, even **k** and **i**. Score all lines, fold dotted lines inward, fold solid lines in opposite direction, and crease neatly.

5 Join same letter tab and triangle edge, starting with **a**, and glue to form pyramids.

6 Color as you wish but in a regular alternating order.

7 When glue is dry, the ring of pyramids is held tightly in the hand to create a flower-like design. Turn ring pyramids one rotation to create a new design. The ring is flexible enough that it can be turned inward or outward. Four different designs can be created.

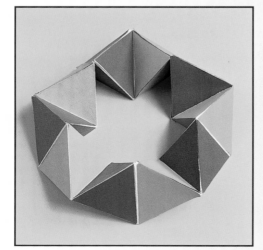

Challenge
The ring constructed above has eight pyramids. A particularly attractive ring of ten pyramids can be made in a similar manner using the same pattern but adding four extra triangle faces to each row.

14

Guess the Number Every Time

Have a friend pick a number! You can guess it in an instant when you're told the colors. An amazing feat? Your friends will be fascinated with your mental powers.

Materials Needed
5 colored sheets of paper: red, white, blue, yellow, purple
Photocopy of cards, page 16
Scissors
Paste or glue

Construction

1 Cut a different color paper to fit each of these cards. Label sheets: red–A, white–B, blue–C, yellow–D, purple–E.

2 Paste the colored paper on the back of the numbered cards as coded: red–A, white–B, blue–C, yellow–D, purple–E.

3 Lay the cards, numbers up, on the table and ask the spectator to pick a number but not reveal it.

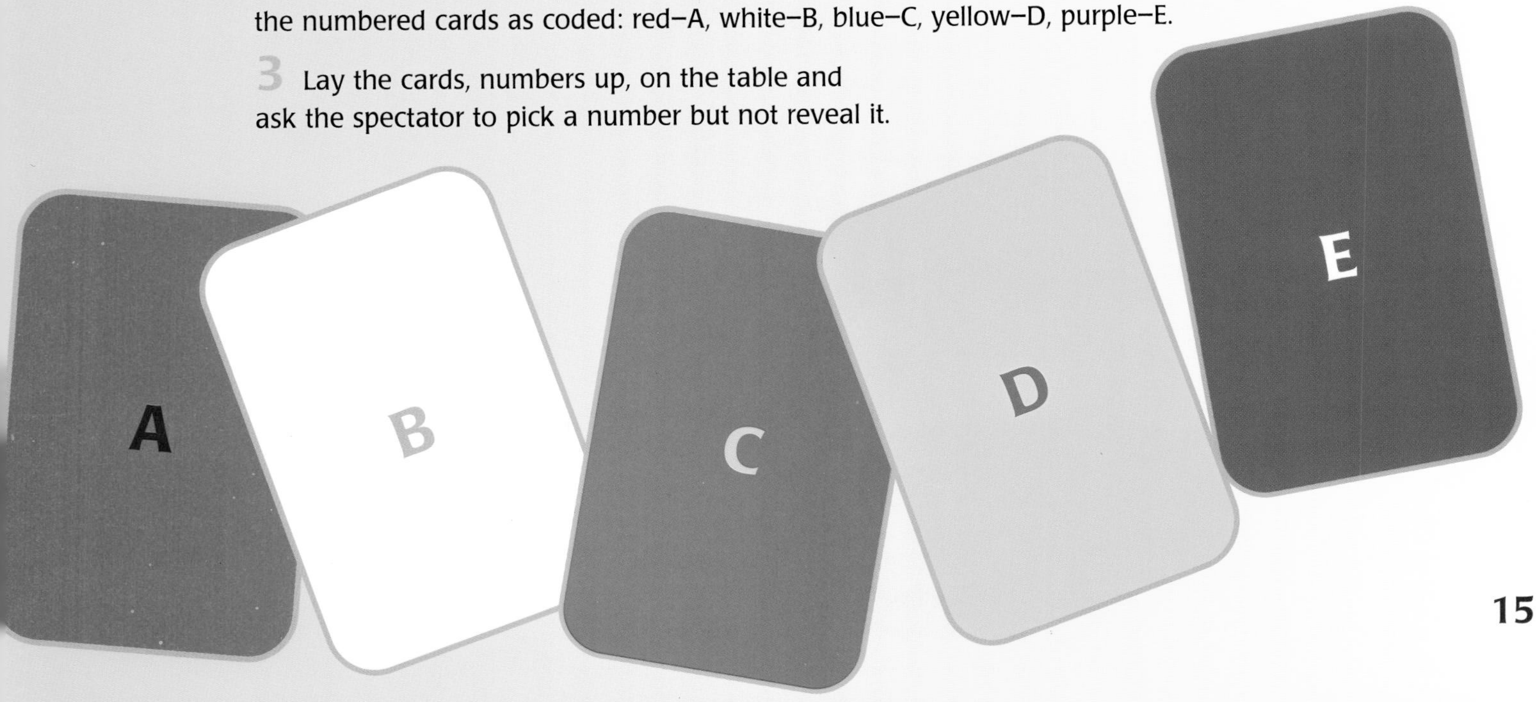

Magical Mind Reading With Numbers

A

B

C

D

E

How to Play

The solution to this trick depends only upon those numbers in the upper left-hand corner of cards **A**, **B**, **C**, **D**, and **E**, respectively. Notice that by adding one or more of these five key numbers, any number from 1 to 31 can be formed in a unique manner. For example, $6 = 4 + 2$; $9 = 1 + 8$; $20 = 16 + 4$; $27 = 16 + 8 + 2 + 1$. Further, there is no other way to form the numbers 6, 9, 20, or 27 using only 1, 2, 4, 8, or 16.

You can guess the thought-of number by two methods.

1 The mind reader must hold up all the cards, and ask the spectator to say "Yes" or "No" to the question "Is your number on the card?" The mind reader then looks at the corner numbers of the cards on which the spectator's number appears. If the spectator's number is on cards **A**, **B**, and **D**, the mind reader looks at the 1, 2, and 8. He adds mentally 1, 2, and 8 (the numbers on the upper left corner of the "yes" cards) and declares that 11 is the thought-of number.

2 This is a more mysterious way to guess the thought-of number. Shuffle the five cards. The mind reader does not look at any numbers while holding the cards with the numbers facing the spectator. He asks the same question: "Is your number on this card?" for each of the five cards. He then reveals the number because he has memorized the color code: red, white, and blue stand for 1, 2, and 4 respectively; yellow for 8; and purple for 16. He then adds the numbers on the "yes" cards that have been memorized from the color code.

A		
1	3	5
7	9	11
13	15	17
19	21	23
25	27	29
	31	

B		
2	3	6
7	10	11
14	15	18
19	22	23
26	27	30
	31	

C		
4	5	6
7	12	13
14	15	20
21	22	23
28	29	30
	31	

D		
8	9	10
11	12	13
14	15	24
25	26	27
28	29	30
	31	

Photocopy card layouts and cut out each card.

E					
16	18	21	24	27	30
17	20	23	26	29	31
19	22	25	28		

16

Counting Blocks Model for Learning Binary Numbers

Any child who can count blocks can learn how to count in the binary number system (multiples of 2) using the model shown with blocks on a board.

Each group of blocks (from right to left) represents the numbers 1, 2, 4, 8, and 16. Using these groups, you can show in a very simple way any number from 1 to 31. For example, show a 5 set by counting the 4 group and the 1 group; show a 7 set by counting the 4 group, the 2 group, and the 1 group; show a 10 set by counting the 8 group and the 2 group.

Using these groups, you will also notice that there is *only one way* to make a 7 set, a 9 set, a 10 set, or any other set up to 31.

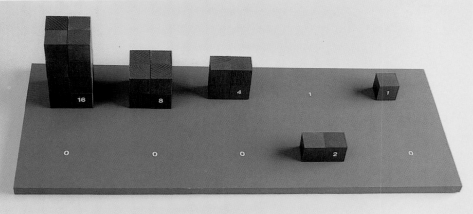

Materials Needed

Wood strip 3 feet (0.9 m) long, 1 in x 1 in (2.5 cm x 2.5 cm) cross section

Plywood 8 in x 20 in (20.3 cm x 50.8 cm) x ½ in (1.3 cm) thick

Saw

Tempera paint or markers

Glue

Sandpaper

Construction

1 Measure and cut thirty-one 1-in (2.5-cm) cubes from the wood strip.

2 Sand all sides of cubes and glue the cubes together into the five different groups, as shown.

3 With markers, color each group, as desired.

4 Divide and mark the plywood into five sections, each 4 in (10.2 cm) wide, as shown.

5 Mark each section with a **1** in the upper portion and a **0** in the lower portion.

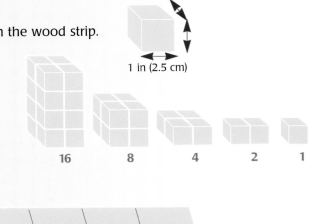

17

6 Place the five groups of blocks in their proper places, as shown. (*Do not glue to the board.*)

How to Use the Blocks and Model

Notice that when we place groups of these blocks on the board according to their values, an amazingly simple thing happens—the binary number equal to each of our numbers appears on the board.

For example, to show 3, count to three by placing the 1 and 2 blocks downward to cover the **0** in their respective sections, as shown. The number reads: 0 0 0 1 1 = binary notation for 3.

To show 4, place the 4 block down to cover the **0** in that section, as shown. The number reads: 0 0 1 0 0 = binary notation for 4.

To show 6, count to six by adding the 4 and 2 blocks. Place the 4 and 2 blocks down to cover the **0** in those sections, as shown. The number reads: 0 0 1 1 0 = binary notation for 6.

Let us now look at the first 11 counting numbers and show how they can be formed using these blocks of cubes. The table on page 19 to the left shows the counting number above and the location of each group of cubes on the board; the table on the right shows their equivalent values in binary notation.

Examine these two tables for the equivalent values of numbers 1 to 11.

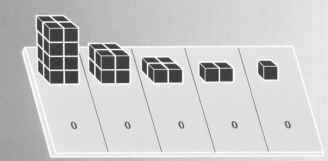

Do not glue blocks to board.

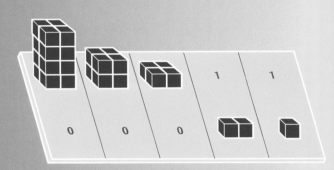

3 = 0 0 0 1 1

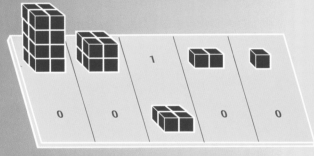

4 = 0 0 1 0 0

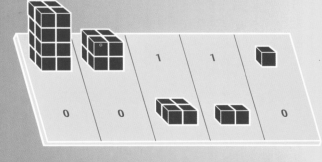

6 = 0 0 1 1 0

Equivalent values of numbers 1 to 11

Binary blocks

16	8	4	2	1
				●
			●	
			●	●
		●		
		●		●
		●	●	
		●	●	●
	●			
	●			●
	●		●	
	●		●	●

Number

1
2
3
4
5
6
7
8
9
10
11

Binary notation

16	8	4	2	1
0	0	0	0	1
0	0	0	1	0
0	0	0	1	1
0	0	1	0	0
0	0	1	0	1
0	0	1	1	0
0	0	1	1	1
0	1	0	0	0
0	1	0	0	1
0	1	0	1	0
0	1	0	1	1

The binary system, like the decimal system, is also a place-value system. The decimal system has values that are multiples of 10: 1, 10, 100, 1000, 10000, etc. The binary values are multiples of 2: 1, 2, 4, 8, 16, etc.

In the decimal system, 24 = two 10s and four 1s. In the binary system, 24 cannot be written with 10s because only 1s and 0s exist. Therefore 24 can only be expressed in multiples of 2, or with values of 1, 2, 4, 8, 16, etc., as shown.

Using the blocks on the binary counting board, you discover that there is only one way to use the blocks to count to twenty-four. You must use the 16 block and the 8 block: 16 + 8 = 24. To express 24 in binary notation, simply bring down the 16 group and the 8 group to cover the **0** in the 16 and 8 sections, as shown. Binary notation for 24 is 1 1 0 0 0.

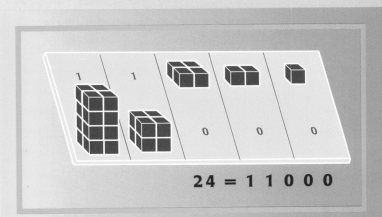

24 = 1 1 0 0 0

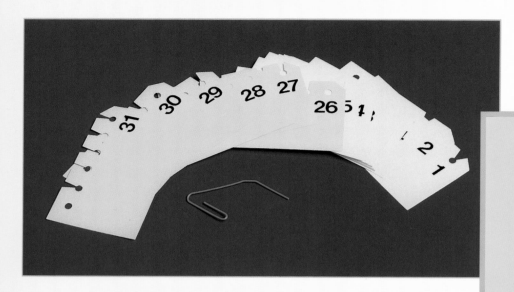

Secret Code Information File

Make your own personal file of computer cards with information about your friends and classmates. Now, by magic, sort out all the boys' cards. When the cards are cut and punched out according to the directions, take a toothpick or wire clip, insert it in the first (right most) hole, and lift the boys' cards from the stack. With a little practice, you can learn to do other surprising tricks with these cards.

Materials Needed

31 index cards 3 in x 5 in (7.6 cm x 12.7 cm), for each file
Hole punch
Marker
Scissors

Construction

1 Mark and cut an angle on the upper right corner of each card, as shown.

2 Make a template, as shown, for punching out all 31 index cards.

3 These six holes on each card represent the 0s in the binary notation. Each counting number has a corresponding binary number. For example, the number 2 expressed in binary form is 0 0 0 1 0. To indicate this on a card, leave the 0s or punched holes as they are, and cut a V-shape where a 1 is present on the number (see examples below).

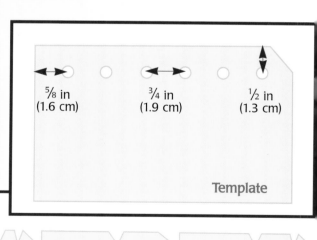

⅝ in (1.6 cm) ¾ in (1.9 cm) ½ in (1.3 cm)

Template

1 = 0 0 0 0 0 1   2 = 0 0 0 0 1 0   3 = 0 0 0 0 1 1   4 = 0 0 0 1 0 0   5 = 0 0 0 1 0 1

4 Proceed in similar manner with counting numbers 6 to 25.

5 After all the cards have been cut, number them and try these experiments.

6 = 0 0 0 1 1 0	16 = 0 1 0 0 0 0
7 = 0 0 0 1 1 1	17 = 0 1 0 0 0 1
8 = 0 0 1 0 0 0	18 = 0 1 0 0 1 0
9 = 0 0 1 0 0 1	19 = 0 1 0 0 1 1
10 = 0 0 1 0 1 0	20 = 0 1 0 1 0 0
11 = 0 0 1 0 1 1	21 = 0 1 0 1 0 1
12 = 0 0 1 1 0 0	22 = 0 1 0 1 1 0
13 = 0 0 1 1 0 1	23 = 0 1 0 1 1 1
14 = 0 0 1 1 1 0	24 = 0 1 1 0 0 0
15 = 0 0 1 1 1 1	25 = 0 1 1 0 0 1

Experiment 1

Shuffle all cards thoroughly, keeping the angle cut of the cards in the upper right corner of the deck. Using an unfolded paper clip wire, insert it in the first hole of the right of all cards. Lift the pack up and shake it so that all the slotted cards drop into your other hand. All the **0** cards will be retained in the clip wire. Look at the number of all the cards in your hand. What do you notice? Look at the numbers of all the cards held on the wire. They are the **0** cards. If you wrote a boy's name on all the cards with the **0** in the first right position, you could quickly sort out all the boys' cards from the girls' cards.

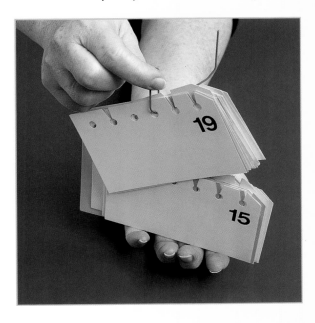

Experiment 2

Shuffle and thoroughly mix all the cards again. Hold the pack in your hand and insert the wire through the first hole on the right. Shake so that all the other cards fall into the other hand. Then place all the **0** cards (those that were lifted and remained on the wire) to the back or bottom of the entire pack. Again, holding the entire pack in one hand, insert the wire in the second hole from the right. Shake so that the slotted cards fall into the other hand again, and place the cards you have now lifted to the back of the entire pack once more. Repeat this operation for the third, fourth, and fifth holes, each time keeping the cards that fall in the hand in order, and the **0** cards retained on the wire placed to the back of the stack. A surprising and magical result takes place. The cards will all be in the proper numerical order from 1 to 31! Try this on your friends and see if you can discover why the mixed-up pack becomes ordered every time.

Experiment 3

Suppose you wish to produce a particular card from the pack, like number 17 or binary number 0 1 0 0 0 1. Take the pack and insert the wire in the right hand slot. Pick up and discard all the **0** cards. Since for card 0 1 0 0 0 1, the 1 is a cut and not a 0, that means the 17 card will drop in your hand with all the other odd cards. Now, holding only those odd cards in your hand, insert the wire in the fifth place from the right where the other 1 is in the binary number for 17 (0 1 0 0 0 1). Lift and discard all the **0** cards again. Now, in succession, put the wire in the second, third, and fourth places of the cards remaining in your hand. Lift and discard those cards that fall in your hand because they represent all the 1s in the second, third, and fourth places. The lone card left on the wire will be card 17. Card 17 has remained because it is the only card in the group that has only the cut slot in the first and fifth positions: 0 1 0 0 0 1.

Magical Mind Reader Window Cards

Materials Needed

Card patterns, page 23
2 sheets light cardboard
Pointed scissors
Paste

Construction

1 Photocopy cards shown on page 23.

2 Cut out the four square cards **A**, **B**, **C**, and **D**. Cut out **E** and **F** as one rectangular piece.

3 Carefully cut out the sections marked "cut out" by puncturing with pointed scissors the rectangular section in the middle and then cutting your way to the edge of the part to be cut. Fold cards **E** and **F** along center line, as indicated, and paste the blank sides together to form the fifth card. With the four cards previously cut and this fifth card, the packet of five square cards should fit exactly upon each other. The cards are now ready to be used. (See solutions on page 24.)

> With no adding or figuring, you can magically produce the spectator's secret number from 1 to 31 after getting "yes" or "no" answers to five questions. This math miracle can be constructed in a few minutes and mastered quickly because the cards are self-working mind readers. No sleight of hand is required. All you have to do is learn simple card handling.

How to Play

1 Mind reader asks spectator to choose a number from 1 to 31 without revealing number to mind reader.

2 Mind reader shows card **A**, **B**, **C**, and **D**, one at a time, and asks the spectator is the number on each card.

3 Mind reader places, in a stack, each card with "yes" answer in upright position (with "yes" in upper left corner), and each card with "no" answer upside-down (all numbers will be upside-down and the cut out square will be in the upper right corner). Mind reader now has a stack of four cards.

4 Take the remaining double-faced card and show side **E**. Mind reader asks the question again, "Is your number on this card?" If answer is "no," turn card **E** 90 degrees so that "no" is in the upright position and place on stack of cards up to puzzle line. If the answer is "yes," place card **E** in the upright position with "yes" in the left corner. Place this card in its proper position, on top of the stack of four cards.

5 Mind reader turns stack of five cards over and the spectator's number magically appears.

Note   When showing cards **A**, **B**, **C**, and **D**, turn only the "no" cards upside-down. When showing card **E**, the "no" card requires only a quarter turn so that "no" is upright. A "yes" answer for card **E** requires no turn.

Photo-copy card layouts and cut out each card. Enlarge, if desired

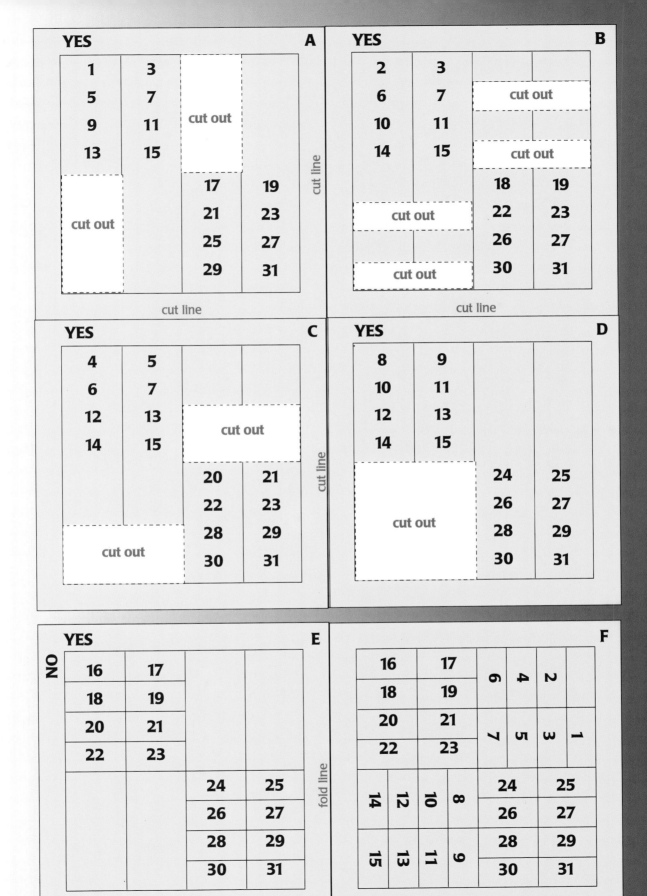

Solution to Magical Mind Reader Window Cards

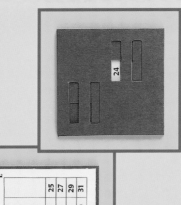

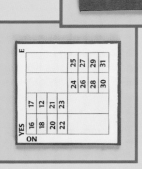

Card F (one side of the folded EF card) is the master card that contains all the numbers from 1 to 31. The windows on cards A, B, C, and D sort out or eliminate the numbers from 1 to 15 much like a computer operates. Card E eliminates all numbers from 16 to 31 if it is turned clockwise 90 degrees to the "no" position. If card E is kept upright in the "yes" position, the chosen number (between 16 and 31) will be revealed when its opposite side, card F, is placed on the window opening left by the first four cards.

Solution to Mental Trick by Adding 1s, 3s, and 9s (Base 3)

Assume the chosen number is seven. The answer to the first question: "Is your number in the first group once or twice?" would be, "Once." The mind reader would then think of "1." To the second question of whether the chosen number is on the second group once or twice, the answer would be, "Twice." Then the mind reader would think of "3" twice or "6." In this instance, the answer to the third question: "Is it in the third group once or twice?" would be "Not there at all." The mind reader thinks of "0." He mentally adds 1 + 6 + 0 = the chosen number 7.

Consider another number: 17. The answers to the three questions would be: "Twice for the first group, twice for the second group, and once for the third group." The mind reader would then add mentally two 1s + two 3s + one 9 = the chosen number: 17.

Any thought-of number can be counted, using these blocks, with one or two 1 blocks, one or two 3 blocks, and/or one or two 9 blocks.

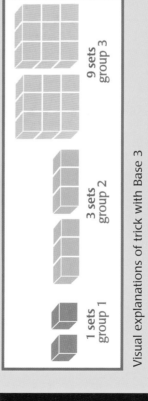

1 sets
group 1

3 sets
group 2

9 sets
group 3

Visual explanations of trick with Base 3 number blocks: 2 sets (1s, 3s, 9s)

Think of 7: This number is in the first group once and the second group twice. Then 1 + 3 + 3 = 7.

Think of 16: This number is in the first group once, the second group twice, and the third group once. Then 1 + 3 + 3 + 9 = 16.

Think of 20: This number is in the first group twice, not in the second group, and in the third group twice. Then we must add 1 + 1 + 9 + 9 = 20.

Mental Trick card– Photocopy card layout on page 25. Cut out and fold as indicated.

Mental Trick by Adding 1s, 3s, and 9s (Base 3)

This mental trick is not found in any math book. This amazing "Base 3" number stunt is so compact it can be put on a business card. It works so quickly that only three questions need to be asked. See the copy of three sets of numbers, shown below.

When showing each of these sets, ask the spectator this question each time: "Is the number you are thinking of in this group once or twice?" The key numbers are those in the upper left corner of each group: 1, 3, and 9.

To guess any number up to 26 or any letter of the alphabet, use this triple-faced card of paper that can be folded in your wallet like a driver's license.

Materials Needed

Pattern, below
Strip of paper 6 in x 2 in
(15.2 cm x 5.1 cm)

Construction

1 Photocopy the pattern numbers on the strip of paper.

2 Fold along fold lines to divide the strip into thirds.

How to Play

1 Ask a spectator to think of a number from 1 to 26.
2 Show the spectator the first group of numbers on your folded card. (The numbers with the 1 in the upper left corner.)
3 Ask the question: "Do you see your number in this group once or twice?"
4 Show the second group of numbers on the folded card, and ask the same question again.
5 Show the third group of numbers and ask the same question.
6 After a simple mental addition you reveal the chosen number.

Hint   Using two groups of the Base 3 numbers (1, 3, 9), as shown, you can now form any numbered group from 1 to 26. You may use any combination of one or two 1s, one or two 3s, or one or two 9s. (See solutions on page 24.)

1	10	19		3	12	21		9	15	21-21
2-2	11-11	20-20		4	13	22		10	16	22-22
4	13	22		5	14	23		11	17	23-23
5-5	14-14	23-23		6-6	15-15	24-24		12	18-18	24-24
7	16	25		7-7	16-16	25-25		13	19-19	25-25
8-8	17-17	26-26		8-8	17-17	26-26		14	20-20	26-26

Three Questions Make Number Magic

This project improves on the previous project. After showing each card, and asking the same question: "Do you see your number once or twice?" stack the three cards together to form one triangular window. Place the stack upon the master card, and the thought-of number appears magically in the window.

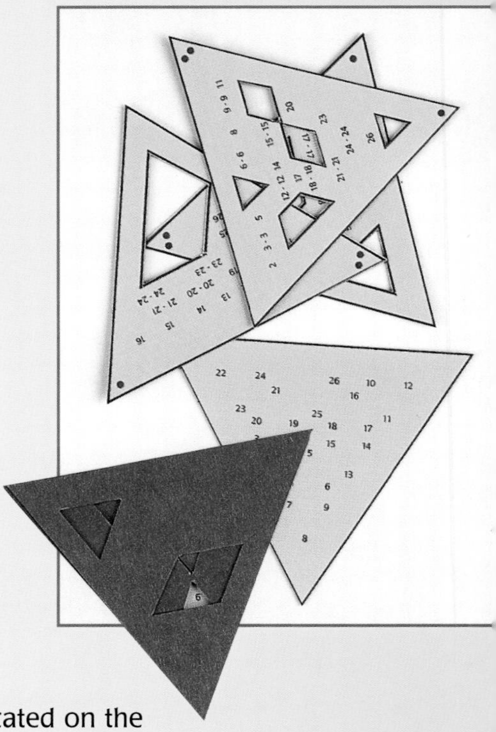

Materials Needed

Patterns of master card and three playing cards, page 27
Heavy paper or card stock
Scissors

Construction

1 Photocopy the four equilateral triangles on page 27, on heavy paper. If desired, enlarge triangles when making copy.

2 Cut out the triangles.

3 Carefully cut out the triangles and quadrilaterals that are indicated on the three playing cards.

How to Play

1 Ask a friend to think of a number from 1 to 26.
2 Note that on each playing card, some of the numbers may not be there, may appear once, or may appear twice.
3 Note also, at each angle of the cut-out triangles of the playing cards, there is either one mark, two marks, or no marks. These indicate which angle of each card will point toward you. Note the positions shown below.

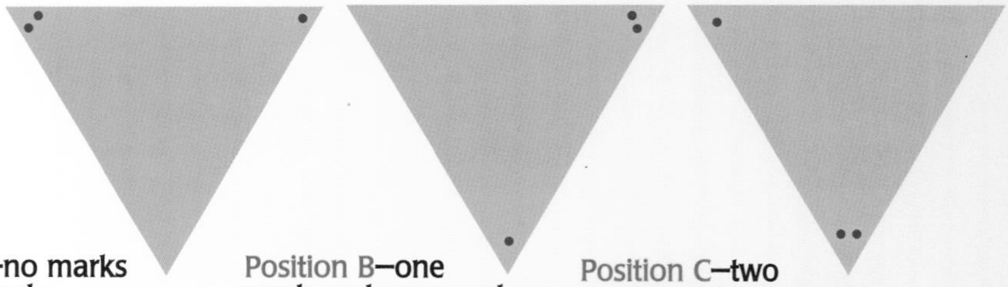

Position A—no marks on lower angle

Position B—one mark on lower angle

Position C—two marks on lower angle

4 Show one of the playing cards. Ask the question, "Do you see your number on this triangle once or twice?" If the answer to the question is: "Number is not there," place the triangle flat, as in Position A; that is, with the angle having no marks on it pointing downward. If the answer to the question is: "I see the number once," place the card, flat as in Position B; that is, with the angle having one mark on it pointing downward. If the answer to the question is: "I see the number twice," the card is placed as in position C with the angle having two marks pointing downward.

5 Repeat this procedure with the other two playing cards in the same manner.
6 When the three triangles are stacked according to the answers in steps 4 and 5, the packet of three cards will form one small triangular window.
7 Place the master card with the numbers upright and with the 8 in the lowermost position.
8 Place the stack of three playing cards, with their numbers facing down, upon the master card to reveal the friend's thought-of number in the small triangular window.

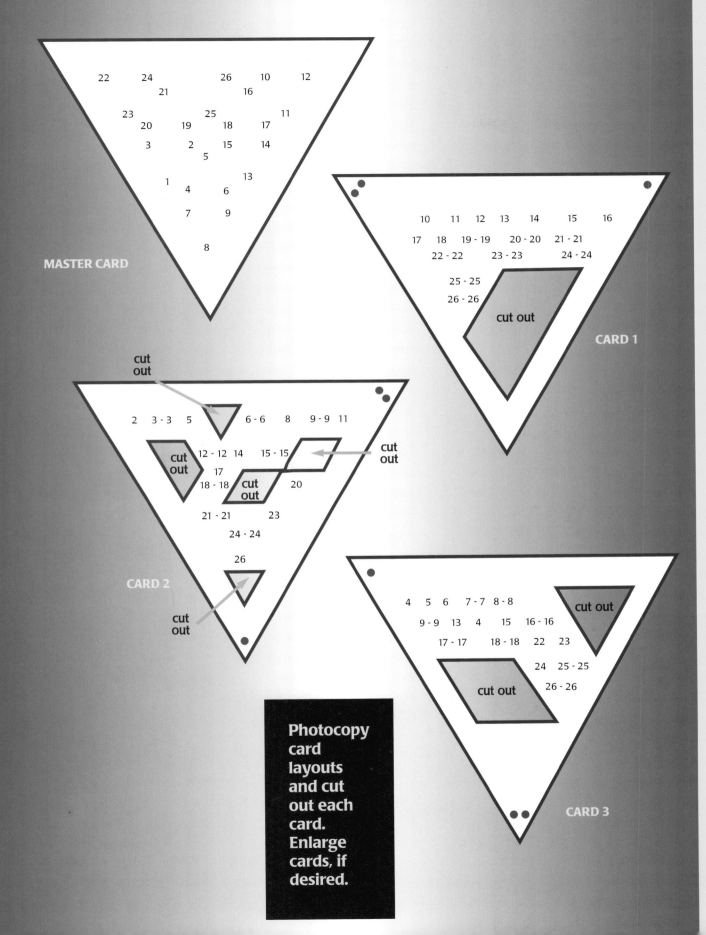

MASTER CARD

22 24 26 10 12
21 16
23 25 11
20 19 18 17
3 2 15 14
5
13
1 4 6
7 9
8

CARD 1

10 11 12 13 14 15 16
17 18 19 - 19 20 - 20 21 - 21
22 - 22 23 - 23 24 - 24
25 - 25
26 - 26
cut out

CARD 2

cut out

2 3 - 3 5 6 - 6 8 9 - 9 11
cut out
12 - 12 14 15 - 15
17
18 - 18 cut out 20
21 - 21 23
24 - 24
26
cut out

cut out

CARD 3

4 5 6 7 - 7 8 - 8
9 - 9 13 4 15 16 - 16
17 - 17 18 - 18 22 23
24 25 - 25
cut out
26 - 26
cut out

Photocopy card layouts and cut out each card. Enlarge cards, if desired.

Solitaire Challenges in Math

Figures with Seven Tans; Pictures with Fourteen Tans

Though this ancient Chinese puzzle goes back thousands of years, and hundreds of original shapes and figures for it have been produced, modern day students and adults continue to be fascinated by the many more geometric shapes, puzzles, and pictures that appear in books and toy stores year after year. The original construction of seven tans from a 5-in (12.7-cm) square piece of thin plywood (pieces labeled I through VII) illustrates how easily and accurately several sets of tangrams can be produced for the few cents it costs to buy thin plywood and sandpaper. With several sets made, these tans are an ideal pastime for birthday parties or group contests.

Materials Needed

Heavy cardboard or thin plywood, 3/32 in (0.2 cm) thick
Paper cutter or fine saw
Sandpaper
Ruler
Pencil

Construction

1 Using paper cutter or saw, cut a 5-in (12.7-cm) square from heavy cardboard or thin plywood.

2 Cut square in half, diagonally, as shown.

3 Cut one of triangle halves to form triangles **I** and **II**, as shown.

4 With other triangle half, locate midpoints **a** and **b** on the two sides of the right angle, and draw a line, as shown.

5 Cut along **ab** to form small triangle **III**.

6 With the remaining trapezoid shape, mark **e** and **f**, and join with ruler. Mark **c** midway between **e** and **g**, and **d** midway

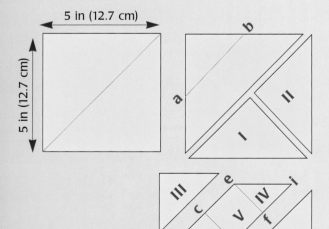

between **h** and **i**. Join **cd**. Cut along the lines to form a small triangle and a square **IV** and **V**, as shown.

7 With the remaining piece, draw a line **jk** to form a parallelogram and small triangle **VI** and **VII**, as shown.

8 Paint or color your tangram pieces, if desired.

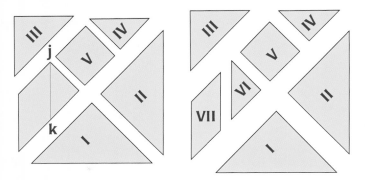

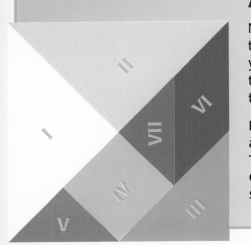

Activity

Now you can prove that the whole square is equal to the sum of its parts. Study the square diagram at left. Imagine cutting the tangram pieces of the square as you would cut a cake. The upper half of the square has been cut in half again to form the large triangles **I** and **II**. Since they are each one quarter of the cake, they are one quarter of 25 sq in (161.3 sq cm) or 6¼ sq in (40.3 sq cm) each.

Figure out the remaining fractional parts and areas for pieces **III**, **IV**, **V**, **VI**, and **VII**. The sum of all the fractional parts should equal 1. The sum of all the areas of pieces should equal 25. (See solutions on page 31).

Tangram Piece	Fractional Part	Area of Piece
I	¼	6¼
II	¼	6¼

Challenge 1

Using the seven tans for each figure, construct the right triangle, the four quadrilaterals, the pentagon, and the two hexagons shown in the diagram. Don't discourage easily. All shapes can be made.

Challenge 2

Next try even more challenging picture shapes below.

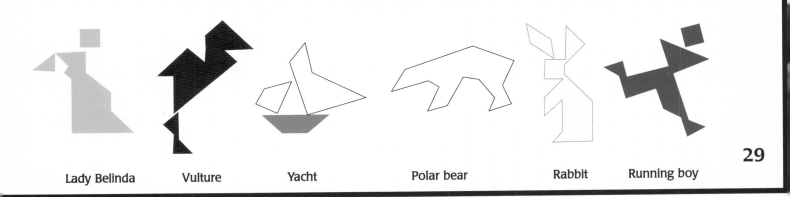

Lady Belinda   Vulture   Yacht   Polar bear   Rabbit   Running boy

Challenge 3

Construct these two sets of figures using two tangram sets.

Mother pushing baby carriage   Ballplayer sliding into home

Challenge 4

Each of the pairs of figures below must be constructed using all seven tans for each figure. Don't give up!

Challenge 5

Arrange and letter the seven tans, as shown. Then rearrange these same pieces, as shown. Notice that under square **D**, there is a large hidden section of triangle **G**. It is the dotted triangle in illustration 2. Why is this area left over?

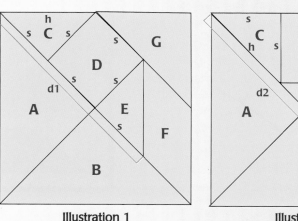

Illustration 1   Illustration 2

Hint   Is illustration 2 a perfect square? Compare the two sides of smaller triangles **C** and **E** plus the side of the square (length **d1**) in illustration 1 with the combined lengths of the two hypotenuses of the small triangles (length **d2**) in illustration 2. (See solutions on page 31.)

Challenge 6

What other figures can you make using the seven tans?

30

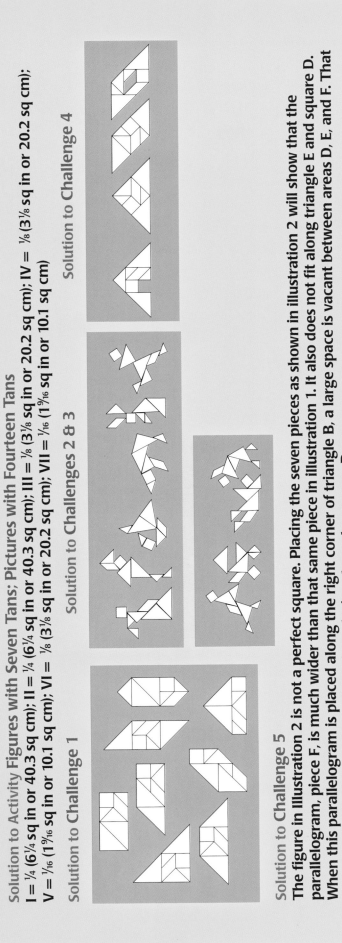

Moving the Tower of Hanoi— The Quick Way

In the legend called The Tower of Hanoi at the great Temple of Benares, three diamond needles were fixed on a brass plate. Sixty gold discs of diminishing size were placed on one needle, and it was called The Tower of Brahma. The problem was to transfer the discs from one needle to another according to two special rules. In this activity, the tower to be constructed is a neat and simple version of The Tower of Brahma with only five square blocks, as shown.

"Moving the Tower" is a fun exercise for children and adults. A very surprising solution for moving the blocks quickly is hinted at in the illustration on page 32.

Materials Needed

Wood, 10 in x 4 in x ¾ in
    (25.4 cm x 10.2 cm x 1.9 cm) thick
Pre-finished plywood, 12 in x ¼ in
    (30.5 cm x 0.6 cm) thick
3 pieces of doweling, each 4 in x 3/16 in
    (10.2 cm x 0.5 cm) thick
Sandpaper
Hand saw
¼ in (0.6 cm) drill with 3/16 in (0.5 cm) drill bit
Clamp
Linseed oil, shellac, varnish, or paint, if desired

Construction

1 Measure three points on the wood block,

31

Solution to Moving the Tower of Hanoi—The Quick Way

Strange as it may seem, an amazing, yet simple solution to the fairly difficult Tower puzzle is found on the scale of the common inch ruler. The enlarged scale of one inch on an ordinary ruler is shown on page 32. Each of the fraction divisions are numbered starting with one for the smallest, two for the next largest, and up to five for the successively larger ones, as shown.

Notice also that the blocks shown here are numbered to size: one for the smallest, two for the next, up to five for the largest.

The steps for moving the first three blocks are listed below:

1 The first two moves are shown in A. Block one goes on the middle post and block two on the right post.

2 The next two moves are shown in B. Block one goes on the right post, and block three goes on the middle post. Note also, on the ruler scale above: 1, 2, 1, and 3—the identical order of the first four moves in the first two steps: 1, 2, 1, and 3.

3 The next two moves are shown in C. Block one on the left post on top of block four, and block two on the center post on top of block three. This permits block one to be moved onto block three and block two. Then block four can be moved to the far right post, as shown in D.

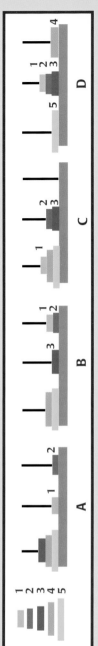

A   B   C   D

Solutions to Challenge 1

To move two blocks takes three moves. $(2 \times 2 - 1)$ or $2^2 - 1 = 3$
To move three blocks takes seven moves. $(2 \times 2 \times 2 - 1)$ or $2^3 - 1 = 7$
To move four blocks takes fifteen moves. $(2 \times 2 \times 2 \times 2 - 1)$ or $2^4 - 1 = 15$
To move five blocks takes thirty-one moves. $(2 \times 2 \times 2 \times 2 \times 2 - 1)$ or $2^5 - 1 = 31$

The pattern, as one can see is two raised to the power of the number of blocks to be moved, minus one. The power of two means the number of times two is multiplied by itself: 2^4 means $2 \times 2 \times 2 \times 2$ or 16.

To move six blocks takes sixty-three moves. $(2^6 = 64 - 1 = 63)$
To move seven blocks takes one hundred twenty-seven moves. $(2^7 = 128 - 1 = 127)$
To move eight blocks takes two hundred fifty-five moves. $(2^8 = 256 - 1 = 255)$
To move "n" blocks requires $2^n - 1$.

as shown on page 33.

2 Drill holes at the three points and insert one dowel in each hole.

3 Measure and cut five squares from the pre-finished pieces of plywood, as shown.

4 Draw two diagonals lightly on each square piece to find the center. Make starter hole on the center, clamp all five pieces together to form a pyramid tower, and drill through all five pieces at one time with a 3/16 in (0.5 cm) drill bit. Remove clamp.

5 Sand edges of all squares, the large wooden block, and the dowels.

6 Finish with linseed oil, shellac, or varnish. Allow to dry. If you have used pre-finished paneling, you may not need varnish or shellac. If color is desired, paint pieces and allow to dry.

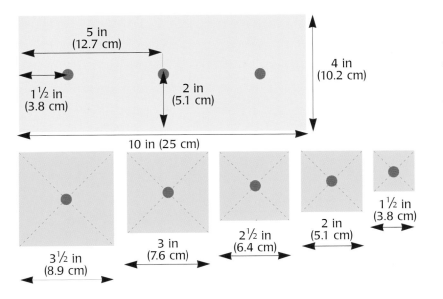

5 in
(12.7 cm)

1½ in
(3.8 cm)

2 in
(5.1 cm)

4 in
(10.2 cm)

10 in (25 cm)

3½ in
(8.9 cm)

3 in
(7.6 cm)

2½ in
(6.4 cm)

2 in
(5.1 cm)

1½ in
(3.8 cm)

How to Play

The object is to move the tower of blocks from the center dowel to one of the other dowels, using a minimum number of moves, according to these two rules:

1 Move only one block at a time.

2 You cannot place a larger block on top of a smaller block at any time.

Hint   A good start at solving this problem is to move a tower of two blocks to another spot. This takes only three moves. Now take three blocks and move them in the least number of moves. Continue with four and then with five blocks, keeping a record of minimum moves necessary.

Challenge 1

After having experimented with the blocks and finding the number of moves for five blocks, you should have discovered a pattern. How many moves are required for six blocks, seven blocks, and eight blocks? Can you discover the rule for any or "n" number of blocks? Do you see any connection between the enlarged one-inch ruler scale shown here and the tower moves? Not only is it an amazing coincidence, but a remarkable key to the move solution. Can you discover this connection?

Hint   Notice the lengths of the ½ in mark, the ¼ in mark, and the other smaller fractional inch marks.

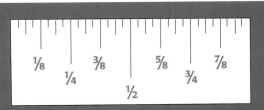

Enlarged scale of one inch on a ruler

Challenge 2

When you have mastered the puzzle moves, an additional challenge of hand-eye coordination is to be able to move the stack of five blocks in less than forty seconds. With a little thought and practice ten-year-olds can do it easily. (See solutions on page 32.)

Figures, Steps, and Walls with Soma Cubes

The Soma Cubes project gives the maker the satisfaction of working with solids much like Lego blocks. Though not as rigid as Lego structures, the seven Soma pieces allow the builder more variety in making many different animals and structures. These wooden models are sturdy and lasting.

Materials Needed

Wood strip about 30 in (76.2 cm) long by 1 in x 1 in (2.5 cm x 2.5 cm) cross section
Saw
Sandpaper
Wood glue

Construction

1 Measure and cut twenty-seven 1-in (2.5-cm) cubes. If you have access to a power saw, cuts will be more accurate.

2 Glue three cubes together to make an L shape, as shown at right. Make six more L shapes in the same manner.

3 Glue one more cube to each of these six L shapes at the appropriate faces, as shown in the other six figures. Allow to dry.

4 Sand all faces of these figures. You will have seven Soma pieces.

Soma Cube configurations

Challenge 1

The seven Soma pieces, made up of twenty-seven cubes, can be assembled to form a larger cube measuring 3 in x 3 in x 3 in (7.6 cm x 7.6 cm x 7.6 cm). When you have succeeded, try finding three other ways.

Challenge 2

Consider if this large cube were painted, what would happen to the small

3 in (7.6 cm)
3 in (7.6 cm)
3 in (7.6 cm)

cubes? Without actually painting, see if you can visualize the number of painted faces each cube would have. Now mark the large cube lightly with chalk. Were your figures correct? Try to put the cube together again so that none of the colored chalk shows.

Challenge 3

An interesting construction problem involves building a tower seventeen cubes high. It is a simple matter to build a tower sixteen cubes high without toppling. But it is not an easy task to build a seventeen cube structure without external support. The first two pieces may be placed, as shown. Impossible? No, it can be done!

Position of first two pieces

Challenge 4

Try to create the block animals below.

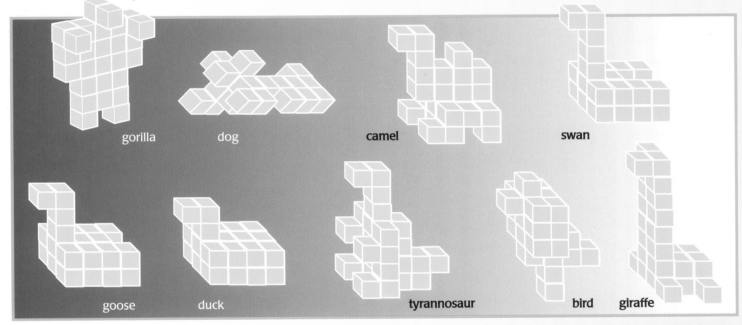

gorilla   dog   camel   swan

goose   duck   tyrannosaur   bird   giraffe

Animals created by Rev. John W. Morgan

Challenge 5

Try these three delightful Soma structures. The penthouse has a cubical hole at its center and is fairly easy to construct. The tower is flat on its invisible sides and has interior holes. The stairway also has three interior holes but, like those of the tower, are invisible from all angles. These are not easy to construct but rewarding if you succeed.

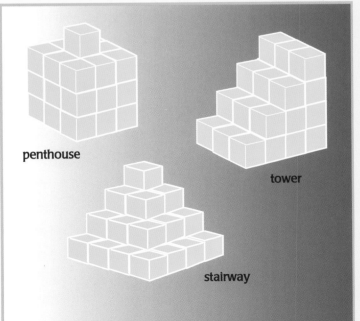

penthouse

tower

stairway

Structures created by Benjamin I. Schwartz

35

Solution to Figures, Steps, and Walls with Soma Cubes

No. of faces painted	0	1	2	3	4	5	6
No. of small cubes	1	6	12	8	0	0	0

Challenge 2   In the large cube, measuring 3 in x 3 in x 3 in (7.6 cm x 7.6 cm x 7.6 cm), if the twenty-seven smaller cubes were painted as one block, certain cubes would have a particular number of faces painted. The answers are in this table.

Challenge 3   This piece is the key to place on the tower. This piece always tends to topple when placed in an upright position on a flat surface. In other words, if it is placed as in the illustration (two cubes high), it does not tip over. But if it is placed three cubes high, it is top-heavy and topples over. If however, it is placed last, a little off the edge, on top of the other six pieces, which stack easily fourteen cubes high, then this last piece, three cubes high, will stand a little on an angle making the tower seventeen cubes high. The secret is in placing this last piece in a slightly tilted position so that it leans like the Tower of Pisa, and does not fall over.

The "1980" or Eighteen Puzzle

Twenty years ago, a game called "Instant Insanity" defied millions of puzzle solvers. Four cubes with four different colors on their faces were arranged in a row so that no one color was duplicated on each of the four visible surfaces. I have altered this puzzle by changing the four colors to four different numbers: 1 - 9 - 8 - 0. The problem is the same as the original whose object is to arrange the row of these four numbered cubes so that each side adds up to the sum of eighteen. The two examples shown in the photographs below show possible arrangements that add up to eighteen. In fact, many times you can arrange to have three of the visible sides add to eighteen, only to find that the fourth side does not. But it can be done!

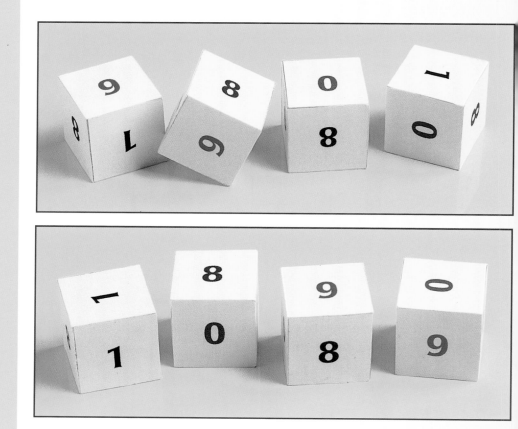

Materials Needed

Strip of wood 4 in (10.2 cm) by 1 in x 1 in (2.5 cm x 2.5 cm) cross section

Saw

Sandpaper

4 different color markers

Construction

1   Saw four 1 in (2.5 cm) cubes from the strip of wood. Sand edges smooth.

2   Mark the digits on the faces of the four cubes, as shown. Use a distinctive color for each of the four digits.

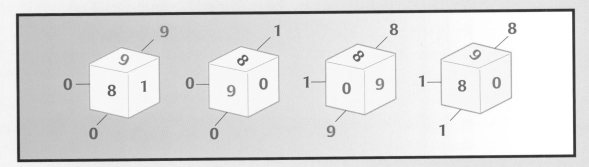

Challenge

Arrange the cubes, four in a row, so that the sum of each visible row equals 18.

Example: 1 + 8 + 9 + 0 = 18, or 1 + 0 + 8 + 9 = 18.

The numbers need not be facing in the same direction but cannot be duplicated.

Magic Trick

Arrange the cubes, four in a row, to form the number 1089. Cover the cubes with paper or handkerchief, and announce that you have predicted, in advance, the answer someone will obtain with a number of one's own choosing.

Have a friend write a 3-digit number (no digits duplicated), reverse the number, and subtract the smaller from the larger. If the number did not change when reversed, have your friend pick another number.

Example: Number chosen   761

Reverse   −167

594

Having done this, have the friend write the answer (in this case 594), and now add it to its reverse (495).

Answer   594

Its reverse   + 495

1089 (final answer)

Uncover the cubes, and show that the prediction matches the final answer. This number trick never fails. Can you figure out why? (See solution on page 38.)

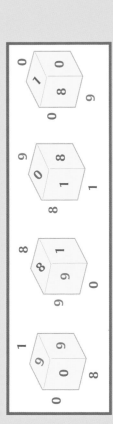

Solution to The "1980" or Eighteen Puzzle

First cube (on left), the one with two 0s and two 9s.

Second cube, the one with two 9s and two 8s.

Third cube, the one with two 8s and two 1s, placed third.

Fourth cube, the one with three 0s, at extreme right.

Explanation for Magic trick

When one subtracts any three-digit number from the larger of that number reversed, the middle digit is always 9, and the ones digit and the hundreds digit will always total 9.

When the answers are reversed, but added, the ones digit and the hundreds will again total 9. The middle digit again is always 9.

The hundreds digit + the hundreds digit =	900	(2+7, 1+8, 0+9, 7+2)
The ones digit + the ones digit =	9	
Middle digit (tens) is always 9, or 9 x 10.		
Therefore, the middle digit always = 90		
Then, the middle digit + the middle digit =	180	(90 + 90)
	1089	(final answer)

Example				Example		
724	321	423	921	297	198	792
-427	-123	-324	-129	+792	+891	+297
297	198	099	792	1089	1089	1089
				297	198	099
				+792	+990	+297
				1089	1089	1089

Exploring Pool Table Difference Triangles

While watching a game of pool several years ago, Colonel George Sincherman of Buffalo, New York, thought of an interesting problem involving the grouping of balls in a triangle as at the start of a billiard game. He called the groupings "difference triangles" where the number of balls in a group were triangle numbers: 3, 6, 10, 15. In illustrations A and B the numbers 1, 2, and 3 form "difference triangles." The number on the bottom ball is the difference between the two numbers on the balls above the bottom ball. Note the next triangle groups C and D (with numbers 1 to 6), and the next triangle group, E (with numbers 1 to 10).

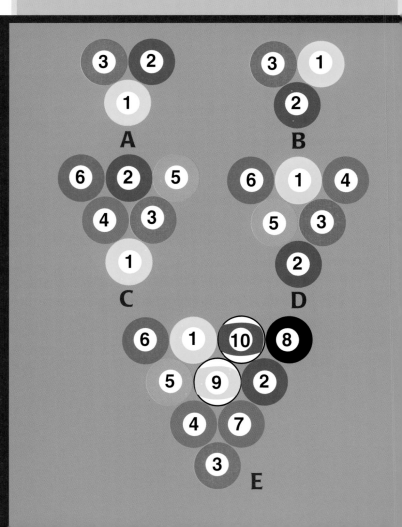

Materials Needed

15-circle layout pattern below
Heavy cardboard or corrugated paper 8 in (20.3 cm) square
Ruler
Magic markers
Scissors
Paste

Construction

1 Cut from cardboard a triangle with 7 in (17.8 cm) sides.

2 Set photocopier at 160 percent enlargement and copy the 15-circle layout.
Paste on the cardboard.

3 Cut out and number fifteen circular markers.
If desired, follow the traditional billiard ball color scheme shown.

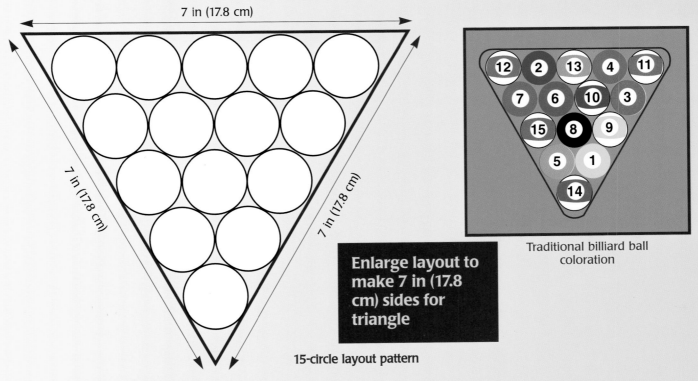

Enlarge layout to make 7 in (17.8 cm) sides for triangle

15-circle layout pattern

Traditional billiard ball coloration

Challenge (Easy)

Form two more difference triangles using the numbers 1, 2, 3, 4, 5, and 6. Form three more triangles using the numbers 1 to 10. These should be fairly easy after a little experimenting.

Challenge (Difficult)

Using the large fifteen-spot triangle you have constructed and the markers you have made, form the one and only difference triangle possible with numbers 1 to 15. Don't discourage easily! Your efforts will be rewarded. (See solutions on page 40.)

Switch'em from One Side to the Other

The name of the game is Switch'em, and the object is to move the red markers to the left, in the places of the white markers while moving the white markers to the right in the places occupied by the red markers. This wooden model with seven pegs on each side to switch unfolds a very interesting number pattern and offers a more challenging problem to solve than similar games with only four pegs on each side.

Materials Needed

Strip of wood 16 in x 2 in (40.6 cm x 5.1 cm) by $\frac{1}{2}$ in (1.3 cm) thick

Dowel 36 in (91.4 cm) long x $\frac{3}{16}$ in (0.5 cm) diameter

Electric drill

$\frac{3}{16}$ in (0.5 cm) drill bit

Sandpaper

Shellac or linseed oil

Red and white markers

Construction

1   Mark center line along length of wood strip. Measure in $\frac{1}{2}$ in (1.3 cm) from one end. Starting at this point, mark fifteen points, 1 in (2.5 cm) apart, along center line.

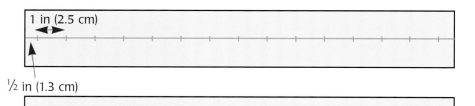

1 in (2.5 cm)

$\frac{1}{2}$ in (1.3 cm)

2   Drill holes at these points with $\frac{3}{16}$ in (0.5 cm) drill bit.

3   Cut fourteen 2 in (5.1 cm) pegs from the dowel. Sand pegs so that they slip easily in and out of the holes.

4   Sand and shellac the finished strip.

5   With markers, color seven pegs red and the other seven pegs white.

How to Play

The object of this game is to transpose seven pegs of one color with seven pegs of the other color according to these rules:

1 The pieces on the right may move only to the left; the pieces on the left may move only to the right. At no time may the pieces change their original direction.

2 A piece may move or jump over a piece of the opposite color in its proper direction to an empty hole.

3 Each move or jump is considered one move.

Hint Begin solving the problem by exchanging one peg with one of the opposite color. (See solutions on page 42.)

Note the number of moves for two pegs is three moves, as shown at left. How many number of moves for four pegs, for six pegs, etc. (See solutions on page 42.)

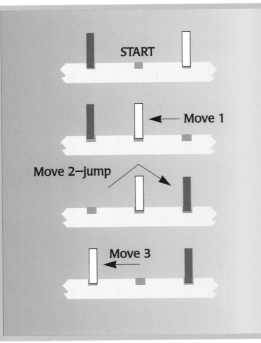

START

Move 1

Move 2—jump

Move 3

Solution to Switch'em From One Side to the Other

First, consider transposing only four pegs, two red pegs with two white pegs. Pegs to move or jump are listed in this order:

red, white jumps, white, red jumps, red jumps, white, white jumps, red (eight moves)

Next, consider transposing six pegs, three red with three white:

red, white jumps, white, red jumps, red, white jumps, white jumps, white jumps, red, red jumps, red jumps, white, white jumps, red (fifteen moves)

Now, consider transposing ten pegs, five red with five white:

red, white jumps, white, red jumps, red, white jumps, white jumps, white jumps, red, white jumps, white, red jumps, red, white jumps, white jumps, white jumps, white jumps, white jumps, red, red, white jumps, white, white jumps, white jumps, white jumps, white jumps, white jumps, red, red jumps, red, red jumps, red jumps, white, white jumps, red (thirty-five moves)

Notice the increasing pattern of moves needed as more pegs are interchanged: 3, 8, 15, 24 (this number was for transposing eight pegs, not in solution above), thirty-five . . .

From 3 to 8 (five more moves)
From 8 to 15 (seven more moves)
From 15 to 24 (nine more moves)
From 24 to 35 (eleven more moves)

As one can now easily see, the increments are in successive odd numbers. For "n" number of pegs to transpose, the rule is: $\left(\dfrac{n}{2} + 1\right)^2 - 1$

Solution to A Child Disappears! Find the Child!

The question, "Where did the missing child go?" is somewhat misleading. The fifteenth child does not actually vanish, for, in fact, parts of it become transformed or joined with several portions of the fourteen children in the second transposition. Upon closer study of the original fifteen children, you will note that several of them are somewhat smaller than those in the second grouping. Notice especially the size of the fourth child of the 15 group, who becomes the thirteenth child of the 14 group. A simple way to explain the vanish is to identify, by name or by number, the original fifteen children. After each child is given a name and number, transpose the two upper pieces. You will immediately see the two names or two numbers on one of the fourteen children.

A Child Disappears!
Find the Child!

This fascinating math vanish has truly confounded many perceptive students. Though not an original, there have been several similar versions of this group of children since this was first printed twenty-five years ago as a cereal box prize. However, figuring out the secret to this vanish is, indeed, not a trivial task.

Materials Needed

Puzzle illustration
Heavy paper or
    thin cardboard
Paste
Markers
Scissors

Puzzle pattern
Enlarge on copier, if desired

Construction

1 Photocopy first group of fifteen children. For sturdier construction, paste the photocopy on heavy paper or cardboard. Color the figures, if desired.

2 Cut on black lines to make three pieces. Letter left side piece **A** and right side piece **B**.

Problem

The original figure contains fifteen children. When you transpose pieces **A** and **B**, as in the lower figure, you find fourteen, not fifteen children! Where did the missing child go? (See solution on page 42.)

Instant Calculations with Number Magic

Add Four 3-Digit Numbers, Faster Than a Calculator

Instant math prowess. This magical trick seems like a miracle. Toss four cubes with different numbers on all faces, and you find the sum immediately, quicker than a calculator or computer! Everyone is impressed.

Materials Needed

Strip of wood 4 in x 1 in x 1 in (10.2 cm x 2.5 cm x 2.5 cm)
Saw
Sandpaper
Marker or crayon

Construction

1 Cut four cubes, each 1 in (2.5 cm) long.

2 Sand thoroughly and round the edges and corners.

3 Copy the numbers on the six faces of each cube as listed below:

Cube 1   642, 741, 543, 147, 840, 345
Cube 2   780, 186, 483, 285, 681, 384
Cube 3   855, 657, 756, 558, 459, 954
Cube 4   773, 179, 278, 377, 872, 971

Solution to Add Four 3-Digit Numbers, Faster Than a Calculator!

Let us simulate three separate tosses of the four dice: Tosses A, B, and C

	A	B	C
First die	642	741	147
Second die	186	780	285
Third die	855	558	459
Fourth die	377	278	179
Totals	2060	2357	1070

(Totals represent sums of tosses A, B, and C)

Notice two significant similarities:

1 The "tens" or second digit of the first die is always 4, the second die is always 8, the third die is always 5, the fourth die is always 7.

2 The second similarity is that since these middle digits are always a 4, 8, 5, and 7, the sum of the tens column will always be 24. (4 + 8 + 5 + 7 = 24)

The simple calculation for obtaining the first two digits of the sum is:

Add the hundreds digit of each of the four numbers to be added; then add the 2 (because the tens column always adds to 24.)

Example For the first toss (A) 642 + 186 + 855 + 377; add mentally 6 + 1 + 8 + 3 = 18

Then add 2: 18 + 2 = 20 (the first two digits of 2060.)

The second two digits of the final sum (2060) are obtained by subtracting the 20 from 80. (Eighty is the key number for all the calculations; that is, for the totals of all tosses, the sum of the first two digits and the last two digits will always be 80.)

Note the answers for the three tosses:

A	2060	20 + 60 = 80
B	2357	23 + 57 = 80
C	1070	10 + 70 = 80

To obtain the second sum: 741 + 558 + 780 + 278, add 7 + 5 + 7 + 2 = 21 + 2 = 23.

Subtract 23 from 80: 80 − 23 = 57. Total = 2357.

Challenge 1

The numbers on the faces of the cubes look like random numbers, but they are not random at all. They are special sets of numbers that can be added easily by a simple mental calculation. Note the tens digit of all six numbers on each cube. What do you also notice about the ones and hundreds digits on each cube?

Toss these cubes ten times. Add the uppermost faces of the four cubes and record the sum of each toss. Study the sums carefully. Each answer has something in common with all the others. Can you discover what makes this magical miracle?

Challenge 2

The numbers on the faces of the cubes are particular sets of numbers designed to be added easily by a simple mental calculation.

Examine the six numbers on any cube. What do you notice about the middle (10s) digit of each cube?

Toss the four cubes as you would toss four dice. Add the four topmost numbers and record the sum. After tossing the cubes and recording the sum about ten times, study the sums carefully.

Each sum has something in common with all the others. Can you discover it?

Hint   Almost all these sums are four digits. Break the four digits into two pairs.

Challenge 3

After discovering the secret to the instant sum trick, see if you can make another set of five cubes with your own groups of numbers.

Solutions to Guess the Hidden Sum with a Diagonal Move

The first clue to discovering immediately the sum of any four covered numbers is to use the number 65, the sum of any row, column, or diagonal on this magic square.

The second clue is to discover the key number that is always subtracted from 65 to obtain the answer of the sum of any four covered numbers.

Consider these two examples of four covered numbers:

Four in the upper right corner of the square

20	7
21	13

15 ⟍ 4

Key number for 1st group   4

Four in the lower left corner of the square

21   Key number for 2nd group

15 ⟍

12	4
18	10

The key number is located by drawing a diagonal line and extending it one and one-half squares from the group of four covered numbers. Notice that there is only one way you can move two spaces diagonally from the four number group without going off the square.

For the numbers in the upper right corner: go down to the second diagonal number: 4.
For the numbers in the lower left corner: go up to the second diagonal number: 21.
The simple subtraction for obtaining the sum is: for the first group   — 65 − 4 = 61.   (20 + 21 + 7 + 13 = 61)
                                                for the second group — 65 − 21 = 44. (12 + 18 + 4 + 10 = 44)

Solution to Instantly Memorize 25 7-Digit Phone Numbers

To obtain the first two digits of a 7-digit phone number, take any of the two-digit numbers chosen. Reverse those two digits and mentally subtract 11.

Example: 38 becomes 83. Subtract: 83 − 11 = 72 (the first two digits)
            73 becomes 37. Subtract: 37 − 11 = 26 (the first two digits)

After the first two digits are obtained, add two digits successively from left to right until you have seven digits.
Follow this sequence: Take 72 (the first two digits in first example). Add 7 + 2 = 9.
Number now is 72 and 9 or 729.
Add last two digits again: 2 + 9 = 11. (Note: if the sum is greater than 9, drop the tens digit or 1.)
Number is now 7291.
Add the last two digits again: 9 + 1 = 10. Drop the 1.
Number now is 72910.
Add last two digits: 1 + 0 = 1.
Number is now 729101.
Add last two digits: 0 + 1 = 1.
Number is 7291011.
The complete number is 7291011.

Break up the number as if it were a phone number: 729-1011.

Guess the Hidden Sum with a Diagonal Move

You can really perform instant calculation on this magic square. As soon as any four numbers are covered, you immediately announce the sum of those covered numbers like a performing mentalist.

Materials Needed

Magic square pattern
Light cardboard
Magic marker
Paste
Compass
Scissors

Construction

1 Photocopy magic square pattern enlarging pattern 125 percent.

2 Cut out square and paste on cardboard cut to fit.

3 Using compass, make a circle 2½ in (6.4 cm) in diameter on cardboard. Cut out.

Challenge

When any square set of four numbers is covered by the marker, the sum of that set can be arrived at immediately by a secret computation with another number.

Hint   Find the magic sum. Cover several groups of four numbers and study the sums. Look for a visible number to subtract. (See solution on page 46.)

1¼ in (3.2 cm)

1¼ in (3.2 cm)

24	11	3	20	7
5	17	9	21	13
6	23	15	2	19
12	4	16	8	25
18	10	22	14	1

2½ in (6.4 cm)

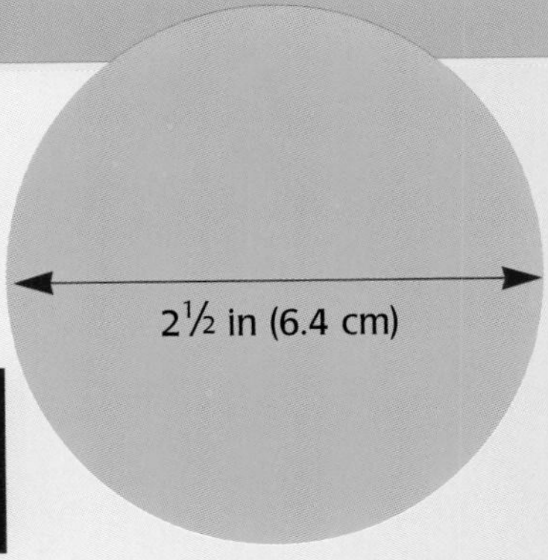

38 **7291011** 729-1011	**73** **2684268** 268-4268	**29** **8190998** 819-0998	**95** **4820224** 482-0224	**48** **7303369** 730-3369
46 **5381909** 538-1909	**34** **3257291** 325-7291	**24** **3145943** 314-5943	**19** **8088640** 808-8640	**76** **5617853** 561-7853
18 **7077415** 707-7415	**74** **3695493** 369-5493	**37** **6280886** 628-0886	**75** **4606628** 460-6628	**58** **7415617** 741-5617
49 **8314594** 831-4594	**63** **2572910** 257-2910	**44** **3369549** 336-9549	**28** **7189763** 718-9763	**33** **2246066** 224-6066
66 **5505505** 550-5505	**84** **3707741** 370-7741	**64** **3583145** 358-3145	**68** **7527965** 752-7965	**53** **2460662** 246-0662

Photocopy card layout and cut out each card.

Instantly Memorize 25 7-Digit Phone Numbers

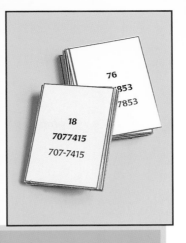

Show off to your friends! Your remarkable phone number memory will amaze them.

Ask the spectator to pick any card from the stack, and tell you the two-digit number on that card. You quickly recite from memory the telephone number on the card that your friend is holding in his hand.

Learn the secret code and you can be a master mentalist!

Materials Needed
Card pattern on page 48
Heavy paper or light cardboard
Scissors

Construction
1 Photocopy page 48 on heavy paper.

2 Cut to size (1¼ in x 1¾ in or 3.2 cm x 4.4 cm) to make a small deck of cards.

Challenge
Have someone shuffle the set of cards, then draw one of the cards, and say aloud the two-digit number of that card.

Since you know the secret code, you can immediately recite the phone number!

If the person, for example, says "75." You respond: "460-6628." What is the secret code?

Hint   Find the relationship between the "key" number and the first two digits of the phone number. (See solution on page 46.)

Solution to Split-Second Multiplication by Cutting a Strip of Paper

Notice the first digit in each of the six possible multiplications:

142857	142857	142857	142857	142857	142857
x1	x2	x3	x4	x5	x6
7	4	1	8	5	2

When the number to be multiplied is turned up on the roll of the die, the person doing the magic mentally multiplies it (1, 2, 3, 4, 5, or 6) by 7 to get the key digit (underlined above).

For example, if the rolled number is 2, multiply mentally 2 x 7 = 14; think 4, the ones or right digit of 14. Then quickly cut the strip to the right of the 4: 14 ✂ 2857. The strip will then read 285714.

Or if the rolled number is 4, multiply 4 x 7 = 28, think 8, the right digit of 28. Quickly cut strip to the right of the 8: 1428 ✂ 57. The strip will then read: 571428.

49

Split-Second Multiplication by Cutting a Strip of Paper

An amazing multiplication feat with the amazing cyclic number: 1 4 2 8 5 7.

A cyclic number is a number obtained by changing a fraction to a decimal that repeats in cycles: $\frac{1}{3}$ (1 divided by 3) = .333333 ... , $\frac{1}{6}$ (1 divided by 6) = .166666 ... , $\frac{2}{3}$ (2 divided by 3) = .666666 .... When the fraction $\frac{1}{7}$ is changed to a decimal, it becomes .142857142857 .... This number 1 4 2 8 5 7, however, is perhaps the most remarkable in our number system. It is the smallest of the cyclic numbers, the only one under a million, with a most unusual property. When it is multiplied by any number from 1 to 6, the product contains the same digits of the original number, (1 4 2 8 5 7), and in the same order!

Note
1 x 142857 = 142857 | 4 x 142857 = 571428
2 x 142857 = 285714 | 5 x 142857 = 714285
3 x 142857 = 428571 | 6 x 142857 = 857142

Materials Needed
Paper strip 11 in x 3 in (27.9 cm x 7.6 cm)
Tape
Marker
Envelope
Die
Scissors

Construction

1 Fold the strip of paper in half and tape the ends of the strip together to form a loop, so it fits into the envelope.

2 Write 1 4 2 in large number size on one half, and 8 5 7 on the other half, as shown.

3 Place the loop in the envelope with the flap of the envelope between the 1 4 2 and 8 5 7, as shown.

How to Play

1 Have the cyclic number 1 4 2 8 5 7 prepared as above. On another sheet of paper write the same number 1 4 2 8 5 7.

2 Hand the spectator a die. Ask the spectator to roll the die to pick the number. Assume the number was 3. Multiply 1 4 2 8 5 7 by 3. The answer is 428571.

3 Announce that the answer was already in the envelope you are holding. Cut the envelope and the enclosed strip, and the answer appears, as shown. How is this done? (See solution on page 49.)

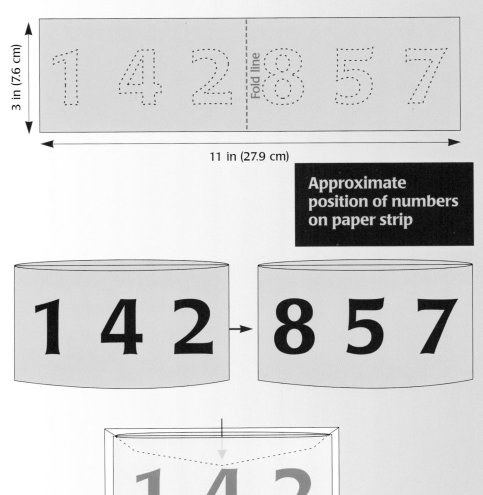

3 in (7.6 cm)

Fold line

11 in (27.9 cm)

Approximate position of numbers on paper strip

1 4 2 → 8 5 7

1 4 2

Slip envelope flap in between the paper strip loop separating the 142 and 857.

Solutions to A Magical Honeycomb

Upon examination of this magical hexagon, you will notice that any 3-cell, 4-cell, or 5-cell row adds up to 38. Examples:

$$16 + 19 + 3 = 38$$
$$12 + 2 + 7 + 17 = 38$$
$$10 + 4 + 5 + 1 + 18 = 38$$

Suppose the 3 and the 19 are covered by a 2-cell marker in the top left diagonal row. The visible number would be 16. To find the sum of the two covered numbers, simply subtract 16 from the magic sum (38): $38 - 16 = 22$.

Suppose the cluster of numbers (3, 19, 7, and 2) is covered by the two 2-cell markers. Notice now that these numbers are parts of two diagonal rows—the 16, 19, and 3 row, and the 12, 2, 7, and 17 row. Since we know that each row in this magic hexagon equals 38, then both rows add up to 2 x 38 or 76. Therefore, by subtracting the visible numbers in those rows: 16, 12, and 17 (their sum is 45), we quickly get the answer: $76 - 45 = 31$. The sum of the covered numbers is $3 + 19 + 7 + 2 = 31$.

51

A Magical Honeycomb

This magical hexagon arrangement of cells is like no other in all of math. Like the queen bee, this honeycomb is one of a kind. The nineteen-cell cluster of hexagons is not only strong and compact, but also allows the most storage in a given space. Knowing the secret of the special numbers in each hexagon enables the mind reader to immediately determine the value or sum of any covered hexagon or pair of hexagons. In fact, the sum of any three- or four-covered row can be quickly ascertained as well.

Materials Needed

Magical hexagon pattern
Heavy paper or light cardboard

Construction

1   Photocopy the magical hexagon below. Enlarge, if desired.

2   Photocopy strips of two, three, and four hexagons. Make two sets. If you enlarge the magical hexagon, enlarge the strips as well.

Challenge

Ask a friend to cover any single, pair, triple, or quadruple group of hexagons. Quickly determine the sum of these numbers. (See solution on page 51.)

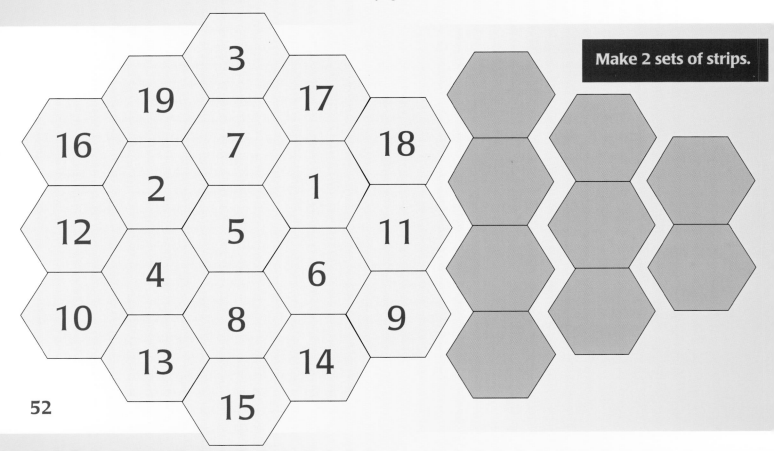

Make 2 sets of strips.

Solids With Many Seats—Made the Easy Way

3-D Math Models to Make

You can make a most interesting mobile without the pain and trouble of cutting and pasting the flaps. Try these constructions. Then color and hang them. You have become a mathematical artist.

The Greeks called these interesting shapes polyhedrons ("poly" and "hedrons," meaning many seats). That is because these solid geometric figures look the same on whatever "seat" or side they are resting. Most geometry books have patterns for the five regular solids shown below, and pupils are often frustrated by the difficulty and time needed to assemble and paste them securely. However, the patterns on pages 54–55 require little or no pasting at all.

Materials Needed

Patterns pages 54–55
Manila folder paper or
   light cardboard
Scissors
Ruler
Glue or paste
Clear tape
Newspaper

Construction

1 Using the photocopy pattern for the cube, cut around the outside and on the solid lines. Score along all dotted lines. (Use a dull scissors edge with some layers of newspaper under the project to make the scoring easier.) Then fold forward and backward along all dotted lines.

2 Tape broken line **AB** on line **CD** inside cube. Start folding flaps along dotted lines to form cube. Finish cube by folding the two longer flaps on top and bottom of cube.

53

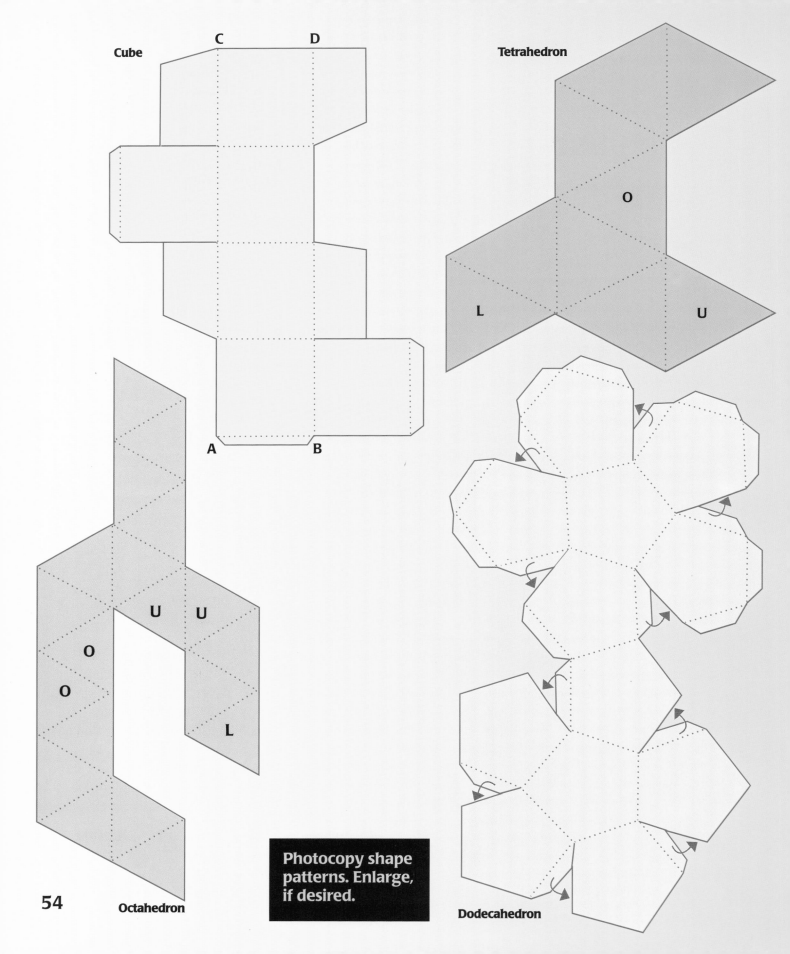

Cube

C   D

A   B

Octahedron

O
O
U   U
L

Tetrahedron

O
L   U

Photocopy shape
patterns. Enlarge,
if desired.

Dodecahedron

3 Using the photocopy pattern for the tetrahedron, cut around the outside. Score the dotted lines and fold.

4 In this construction, triangle **O** goes over triangle **U**. Triangle **L** is tucked in last.

5 Using the photocopy pattern for the octahedron, cut around the outside. Fold on the dotted lines.

6 Start folding triangles as before. The last triangle to tuck in is **L**.

7 Using the photocopy pattern for the dodecahedron, cut around the outside and on the solid lines. Score the dotted lines. Fold.

8 Paste the flaps on the adjacent edge (indicated by arrows) of the pentagon. When this is done for each flap, the dodecahedron is formed by securing both halves upon each other with clear tape.

9 Using the photocopy pattern for the icosahedron, cut out along all solid lines. Cut solid lines within the shape with scissors. Score along all dotted lines and fold.

10 Place glue on top of **U** flaps and under **O** flaps. Triangle **1-U** goes under triangle **1**, **11-U** goes under triangle **11**, etc.

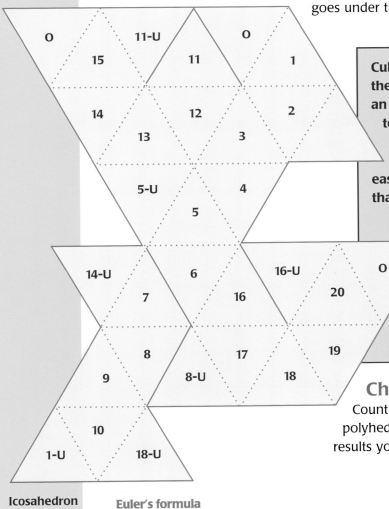

Icosahedron

Cubes are used most commonly as dice today. But all of these solids can be used as dice because each face has an equal chance of appearing on top when the die is tossed. Some of the most popular board games use the octahedron with the numbers 1 to 8 instead of our popular cubic dice. However, we could just as easily use the dodecahedron and icosahedron, a shape that was found two thousand years ago in Egypt.

Because Plato, the Greek philosopher, made the first serious study of the shapes, they are often referred to as the Platonic solids. Much later, the famous Swiss mathematician, Leonhard Euler, found an interesting relationship between the numbers of faces, vertices, and edges for each polyhedron.

Challenge

Count the number of faces, vertices, and edges for each polyhedron. See if you can discover Euler's formula from the results you recorded. See answer at left.

Euler's formula
Number of faces + number of vertices − 2 = number of edges for each polyhedron.

To make the attractive mobile on page 53, cut out a 6½ in (16.5 cm) circle from cardboard. Attach the models with thread and paper clips inside the solids.

This Octahedron Reads Minds

Hold the octahedron like a crystal ball, gaze in it intently, then ask a simple question three times. It sounds mysterious but it will reveal your friend's thought-of number in a second. A third grade student who learns this secret can do this mind-reading trick as well as an adult.

Materials Needed

Octahedron pattern page 54
Heavy paper or light cardboard
Scissors
Transparent tape
Markers

Construction

1 Photocopy the pattern on page 54 onto heavy paper or light cardboard. Cut on the solid lines, score and fold on the dotted lines.

2 Assemble the octahedron by putting the **O** triangles over and the **U** triangles under. The last flap to insert is labeled **L** Tape any loose sides or edges.

3 Number the octahedron in the following way:
   a) Hold it in position 1, as shown, facing you and write the numbers, as indicated.
   b) Rotate the model 90 degrees, toward you. Add numbers 2 and 6 to the two blank faces, as shown in Position 2.
   c) Rotate to the left 90 degrees, as shown in position 3, and add the number 4.
   d) After steps a, b, and c, one side remains blank. Number it 0.

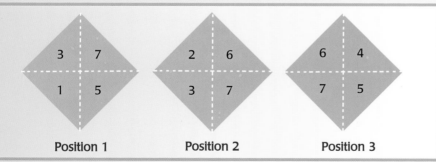

	Position 1			Position 2			Position 3	
3	7		2	6		6	4	
1	5		3	7		7	5	

Challenge

In order to perform the magic, you must memorize the three positions shown in the diagram. Remember that the three positions shown directly face the person on whom you are performing the magic. Ask the person to choose a number from 1 to 7, but not reveal it.

When the numbers 1, 5, 7, and 3 are facing directly toward

The answers to the three questions can be "yes" or "no."

If the answer to the first question is <u>yes</u>, think 1; if <u>no</u>, think 0.

If the answer to the second question is <u>yes</u>, think 2; if <u>no</u>, think 0.

If the answer to the third question is <u>yes</u>, think 4; if <u>no</u>, think 0.

Add the <u>yes</u> answers to the three questions to determine the number your friend had in mind.

Example: If the first answer is <u>yes</u>, and the second and third are <u>no</u>, think: $1 + 0 + 0 = 1$.

If the first and second answers are <u>yes</u>, and the third is <u>no</u>, think:

$1 + 2 + 0 = 3$.

If the first, second, and third answers are <u>yes</u>, think: $1 + 2 + 4 = 7$.

If the first answer is <u>no</u>, and the second and third answers are <u>yes</u>, think: $0 + 2 + 4 = 6$.

the person, you are holding the octahedron so that you can see only the 7 and 3 as you look down at it. Your first question is: "Do you see the number you are thinking of?" The person will answer "Yes" or "No."

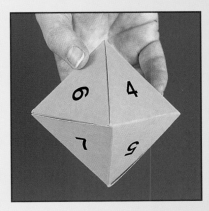

Rotate the octahedron one quarter turn, toward the person you are questioning. The numbers as in position 2 will be facing the person. Again ask: "Do you see the number you are thinking of?"

Now turn the octahedron one quarter turn to the right, and the numbers of position 3 will be directly facing the person. Again ask: "Do you still see the number you are thinking of?" From the answer you can immediately announce the thought-of number.

Hint   There is a binary principle involved. Can you discover it? Look at the three positions shown. If you were thinking of the number 1, how many "yes" answers would you give to the three questions.

If the number was 3, how many "yes" answers?

If the number was 7, how many "yes" answers?

(See solution at left.)

Solution to "He Loves Me" Daisy Puzzle

Challenge   The second player, if playing thoughtfully, usually wins. The strategy is to break the circle of petals into two partial circles that are always symmetrical. Whether the first player takes one petal or two, the second player responds by taking one petal or two from the opposite section of the circle making sure to restore the symmetry. This leaves the remaining ten petals divided into two groups of five petals each. Again, no matter what number of petals the first player removes, the second player restores symmetry by removing the same appropriate number. Finally, when the number of petals is reduced to two on one side and two on the opposite side, the first player can take only one or two of either of the remaining pairs. The second responds by taking two or one, governing his selection so that he leaves the last petal for the first player.

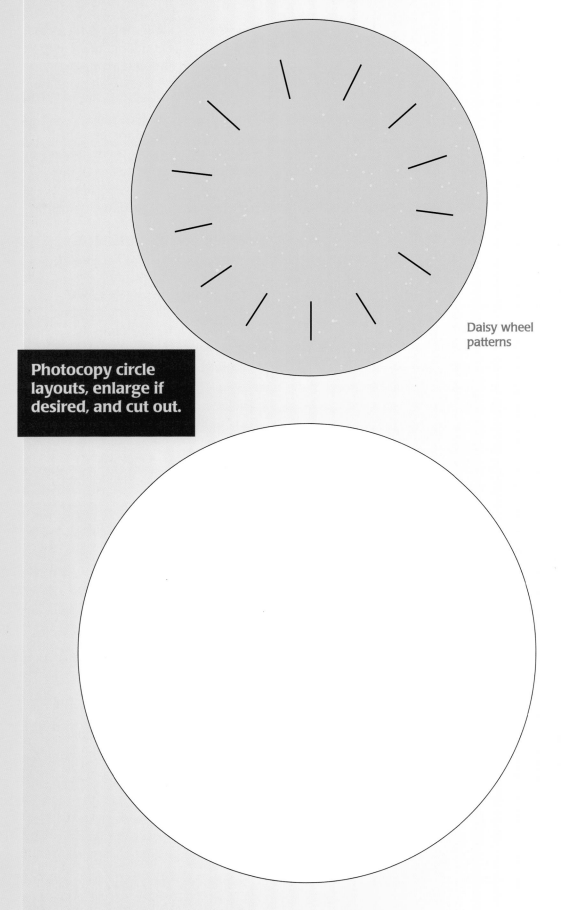

Daisy wheel patterns

Photocopy circle layouts, enlarge if desired, and cut out.

"He Loves Me" Daisy Puzzle

Games- manship in Math

According to romantic legend true love can be determined by removing petals from a daisy one by one while reciting "He loves me" or "He loves me not" alternately as each petal is removed. When the last petal is removed, the phrase being uttered at the time determines whether true love exists.

This game is a slightly different version of the Daisy Game. It takes minutes to make, yet can provide hours of fun and strategy planning.

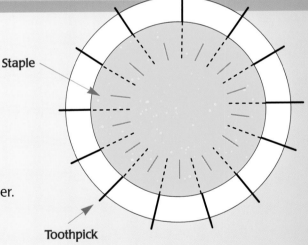

Materials Needed

Pattern for Daisy Puzzle circles on page 58
13 round toothpicks
Heavy paper or light cardboard
Scissors
Stapler

Construction

1 Photocopy the circles on page 58 onto heavy paper. Cut out.

2 Staple small circle on top of larger one using only thirteen staples, one on each black mark.

3 Insert toothpicks between the staples, as shown.

Rules of the Game

1 Each player, taking turns, may remove one toothpick from anywhere on the Daisy or may remove two, but only if they are adjacent to each other (that is, they are next to each other and no toothpicks have been removed in between).
2 The player that takes the last toothpick loses.
3 Players alternate in starting new games.

Challenge

After several games, can you discover who has the advantage, the first player or the second? Why? (See solution on page 58.)

59

Triangles on a Board

This paper and pencil game called Sim owes its origin to Gustavus J. Simmons. The game is played by two persons on the six vertices of a regular hexagon using two colored pencils. This new and original version is played on a square board using two colors of rubber bands on nails and pegs. This board game can be easily cleared when the game is finished by removing the rubber bands to start again.

Materials Needed

Board 7 in x 7 in x ¾ in (17.8 cm x 17.8 cm x 1.9 cm) thick
Dowel 12 in x ⅛ in (30.5 cm x 0.3 cm) thick (optional)
6 brads or finishing nails
Hammer
Rubber bands, 8 red and 8 green
Drill and ⅛ in (0.3 cm) drill bit
Compass

Construction

1 Using a compass, draw a circle with a radius of 3 in (7.6 cm) on the square board.

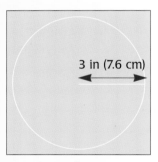

3 in (7.6 cm)

2 Using the same radius, mark six points on the circumference and connect them to form a hexagon.

3 Using the hammer, nail brads or finishing nails at these points. Allow them to stick up above the surface ½ in (1.3 cm).

4 For a more finished board game, ⅛ in (0.3 cm) dowels may be used instead of brads or nails. Drill six ⅛ in (0.3 cm) holes ⅜ in (1 cm) deep at the six points of the hexagon. Cut dowels into six 2-in (5.1-cm) pieces and hammer securely into each hole.

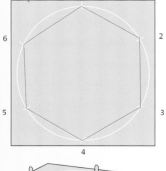

Rules and Strategy

The object of the game is *not* to form a triangle in your color rubber band before your opponent.

1 Each player starts with eight rubber bands of one color.

2 Then, taking turns, each player connects any two of the six points on the hexagon with his particular color rubber band. Since the object is *not* to form a triangle in your color, your strategy is to connect points that will force your opponent to form a triangle in his color before you do.

3 Note smaller triangles formed with a vertex *not* at a point on the hexagon do not count. See the sample game below.

Sample game

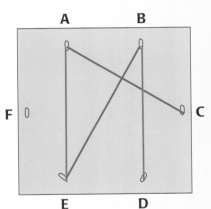

First player stretches his band from **A** to **C**.
Second player connects **A** to **E**.

First player stretches his second band from **B** to **E**. Second player connects **B** to **D**.

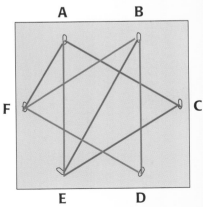

First player stretches his third band from **E** to **C**. Second player connects **D** to **F**.
First player stretches his fourth band from **A** to **F**. Second player connects **F** to **B**.
The second player has lost the game because point **F** was connected to points **B** and **D** to form a triangle.

Challenge 1

After playing a few games, can you determine if it is possible for the game to end in a draw? Why?

Can you find a winning strategy?

Who has the advantage in the long run, the first player or the second?

Challenge 2 (Difficult)

Using this type board in a different manner, see if you can discover this tricky pattern. Study the six circles shown.

Look at circle **A**. When two points are connected, two areas are formed.
Now note carefully:
In circle **B**, when three points are connected, four areas are formed.
In circle **C**, when four points are connected, eight areas are formed.
In circle **D**, when five points are connected, sixteen areas are formed.
In circle **E**, when six points are connected, a surprise occurs. There are not thirty-two areas. Count again.
In circle **F**, as in the previous circles, connect the seven points to all the other points. Carefully count all areas that are formed.
Finally connect eleven points to every other point. See if you can discover a pattern.

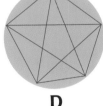

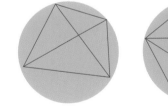

Circle	Points connected	Areas formed
A	2	2
B	3	4
C	4	8
D	5	16

Though this is not an easy exercise, it is worth the effort and will give you a perfect score in problem solving if you succeed! (See solution on page 62.)

Solutions to Triangles on a Board

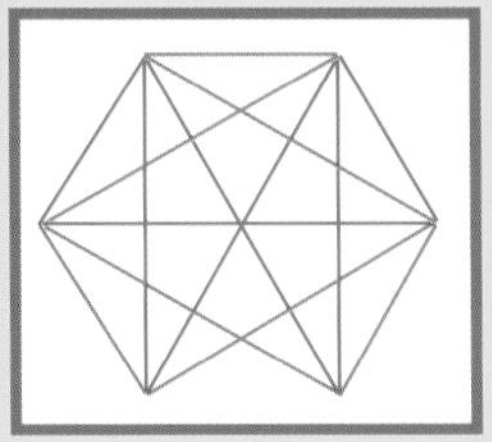

Challenge 1 This game cannot end in a draw. There is only one basic position that allows the game to go fourteen moves without one player forming a triangle of one color. It is similar to the illustration, shown here. Notice that each player has used seven rubber bands of his color. Whoever goes next loses. This means that the player who goes second has an advantage if his seven moves do not form a triangle, because the eighth move will have to form a triangle.

Challenge 2 (Difficult)

The simple pattern 1-2-4-8-16 does not work here. Connecting six points does not form the expected 32 but 31 areas! Similarly, with seven points connected 57 areas are produced. Therefore, another pattern is needed.

Begin as before in Circle A. When you add one segment to the circle you add one area. When you add two more segments as in Circle B, you gain two more areas making a total of four areas. See the table below.

Circle	Points connected	Added segments (total)	Total areas
A	2	1	2
B	3	1 + 1 (2)	4
C	4	1 + 2 + 1 (4)	8
D	5	1 + 3 + 3 + 1 (8)	16
E	6	1 + 4 + 5 + 4 + 1 (15)	31
F	7	1 + 5 + 7 + 7 + 5 + 1 (26)	57 *continue the pattern*
G	8	1 + 6 + 9 + 10 + 9 + 6 + 1 (42)	99
H	9	1 + 7 + 11 + 13 + 13 + 11 + 7 + 1 (64)	163
I	10	1 + 8 + 13 + 16 + 17 + 16 + 13 + 8 + 1 (93)	256
J	11	1 + 9 + 15 + 19 + 21 + 19 + 15 + 8 + 1 (130)	386
		final total	386

Solution to Construct a Bridge of Linking Hexagons

The possibilities of playing the game of Hex on a 6 x 6 unit, 7 x 7 unit, or larger board have never been fully analyzed. There is, however, a distinct advantage for the first player, particularly if that player first occupies the hexagon in the center (the one with the star in its center). Therefore, to offset this advantage, no player may occupy that center hexagon until after the third move. This gives the second player the option of occupying that central hexagon on the fourth move. Because of the tremendous number of possible moves and counter moves, there is no simple formula to win this game every time. The important strategy is to keep the bridge intact, for once the bridge is broken, the possibilities for mending it are quite slim.

Construct a Bridge of Linking Hexagons

Hex was invented by Piet Hein and began its existence in Scandinavian countries. It is a clever game that never ends in a draw. There's always a winner. In this think-ahead adaptation more planning is required.

Materials Needed

Pattern of game board on page 64
Heavy cardboard 9 in x 12 in
    (22.9 cm x 30.5 cm)
Colored pencils or magic markers
Red cardboard, 4 in x 4 in
    (10.2 cm x 10.2 cm)
Blue cardboard, 4 in x 4 in
    (10.2 cm x 10.2 cm)
Paste
Scissors
Compass
Envelope
Stapler

Construction

1 Photocopy the game board pattern. Cut out and paste on the 9 in x 12 in (22.9 cm x 30.5 cm) heavy cardboard. Color, if desired.

2 Color the opposite borders of seven hexagons a distinctive color (red for two opposite borders and blue for the other two hexagon borders), as shown.

3 Using either a compass or circle template, make 30 markers that fit the hexagon spaces, using the two colored pieces of cardboard—15 red circles and 15 blue circles.

4 Staple the envelope on the back side of the game board to store markers when not in use.

Rules and Strategy

The object of the game is to complete a chain of pieces of the player's color from one side to the opposite side.

1 Players alternate placing pieces of their color on any unoccupied hexagon. The central hexagon may not be occupied until after the third move.

2 If a player has red pieces, try to construct a bridge from one red side to the opposite red side. The player with the blue pieces tries to do the same from the blue border to the opposite blue

63

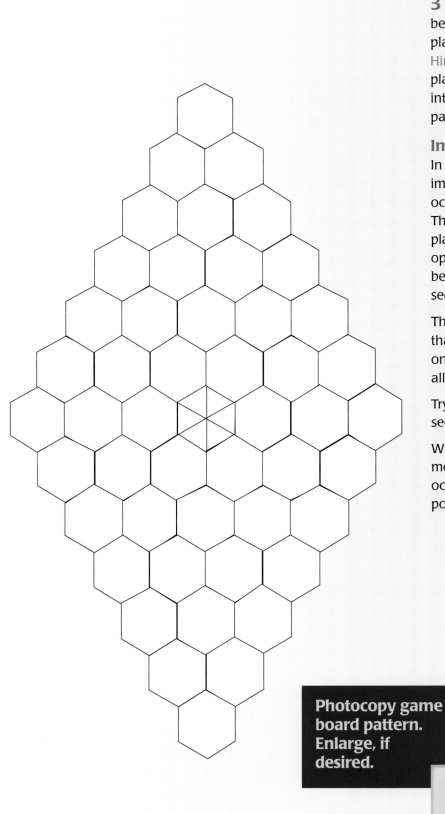

border.

3 The hexagons at the four corners of the board belong to either side, and can be used by either player to make the unbroken chain.

Hint   Once a chain is started, keep it intact and plan ahead to occupy key cells to prevent interception by your opponent. (See solutions on page 62.)

Important points

In this version of the game the central star is important to the game strategy. It may not be occupied until after the third move in any game. This somewhat nullifies the advantage of the first player in that the second player has the first opportunity to occupy the central star hexagon because the fourth move will always fall upon the second player's turn.

The primary objective is to form an unbroken road that connects the battle lines of your color. Place one of your first two markers near the center to allow for more defensive moves.

Try to keep your started chain intact, or with sections of the chain no more than one cell apart.

When attacking, assume the opposite strategy and move to dismember the opponent's chain by occupying intercepting cells left in a vulnerable position.

Photocopy game board pattern. Enlarge, if desired.

Since a tie is impossible in this game, occupying some of your opponent's border cells is a wise move if you can do so without weakening your position.

Tac Tic Take Away

Sixteen pennies and a small piece of plywood can make a game to boggle the mind! This interesting Tac Tic game involves the look-ahead strategy of chess, and surprising moves that can change an apparent defeat into victory. The game in the photograph employs sixteen markers on a 4 x 4 grid board.

Materials Needed

Plywood 4 in x 4 in (10.2 cm x 10.2 cm) by ⅛ in (0.3 cm) thick
Magic marker
Sandpaper
16 pennies
16 red adhesive-backed ¼ in (0.6 cm) dots

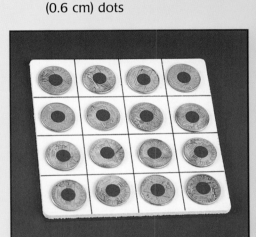

Construction

1 Sand plywood piece, rounding corners evenly.

2 Divide each side into four 1-in (2.5-cm) sections.

3 Connect opposite side with magic marker to form a 4 x 4 grid.

4 Place red dots in the center of each penny and position coins, as shown.

Rules and Strategy

The object is to force the opponent to take the last marker.

1 Each player, taking alternate turns, may remove one to four markers in any row or column.

2 A player cannot take a whole row or column if there are spaces in between. (If row is • •   • or •   •, player can take only one or two in first example or only one in the second example.)

3 If one player goes first in one game, the second player goes first in the next game.

After a few games, one may quickly think that following the opponent's move symmetrically opposite will ensure a win for the second player, but this is not always the case.

Hint   Examine the two illustrated losing positions. The two positions shown at **A** and **B** are hopeless to respond to. That means the next player will surely lose. In **A** the next player can take only one marker. His opponent takes the second one forcing the next player to lose because he is stuck with the last marker. In **B** the next player can take only one or two markers in a row or column. His opponent can respond by taking two if one is taken or by taking one if two are taken. This again leaves one marker for the next player. Therefore, he loses.

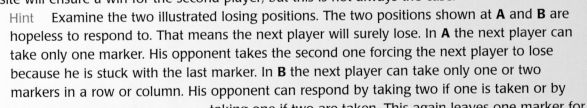

A

B

Challenge

What is a general strategy for winning? See the answer below.

Solution   The strategy is to avoid being trapped into any 1, 1, 1 situation or into any 2, 2 situation.

Make a 5 x 5 grid board and using the same rules try playing this even more challenging game.

Solution to A New Nim Game

The key to winning at Nim lies in knowing whether a position is safe or unsafe. How to determine this involves two steps:

1. Express the number of pegs in each row as the sum of powers of 2. The powers of 2 are: 1, 2, 4, 8, etc.

   Note these examples of three common positions: (5, 6, 7), (4, 5, 1), (3, 2, 1)

$5 = 4 + \underline{1}$	$4 = \underline{4}$	$3 = \underline{2} + \underline{1}$
$6 = \underline{4} + 2$	$5 = \underline{4} + \underline{1}$	$2 = \underline{2}$
$7 = \underline{4} + \underline{2} + \underline{1}$	$1 = \underline{1}$	$1 = \underline{1}$

2. If all these powers (the underlined numbers) now form pairs, the position is safe. Thus the second position, the 4, 5, 1 group, is safe because there they are a pair of 4s and 1s. The third position is also safe because there are a pair of 2s and a pair of 1s. The first position, 5, 6, 7, is unsafe because there are three 4s, not an even pair of 4s.

   Examine these three safe positions more closely.

   ```
   4, 5, 1        5, 6, 1        3, 2, 1
   • • • •        • • • • •      • • •
   • • • • •      • • • • • •    • •
   •              •              •
   ```

No matter what the opponent takes from these three safe positions, the other player can always leave two rows of equal numbers: 4–4, 3–3, 2–2, 1–1, all safe positions. The 5, 6, 7 is an unsafe position.

In order to make this group a safe position, the next player must remove four pegs from any row. Note the following moves were all 5, 6, 7 at the start.

```
x x x x              • • • • • •          • • • • • •
• • • • •            x x x x x            x x x x
• • • • • •          • • • • •            • • • • •
• • • • • • •        • • • • • • •        x x x x
(a)                  (b)                  (c)
with four taken (a)  with four taken (b)  with four taken (c)
changes to 1, 6, 7   changes to 5, 2, 7   changes to 5, 6, 3
```

Since these three positions are all safe ones, no matter what number of pegs the player removes, the first player can always leave two rows of equal numbers and eventually win the game.

Game board pattern

1 in (2.5 cm)

½ in (1.3 cm)

½ in (1.3 cm)

Photocopy pattern. Enlarge 300%.

A New Nim Game

This take away Nim game version has eighteen pegs to challenge the player. It is compact, easy to construct, and offers many surprises for winning or losing!

Materials Needed

Pattern for game board on page 66
Board 8 in x 4 in (20.3 cm x 10.2 cm) by ¾ in
    (1.9 cm) thick
Dowel 36 in (91.4 cm) and 3/16 in
    (0.5 cm) diameter
Magic marker
Drill and 3/16 in (0.5 cm) drill bit
Sandpaper
Shellac, linseed oil, paint (optional)

Construction

1 Photocopy pattern on page 66. Cut out.

2 Place pattern on board and transfer all the points to the board with the magic marker.

3 Drill holes at all these points.

4 Cut eighteen 1½ in (3.8 cm) dowels to fit easily in each hole.

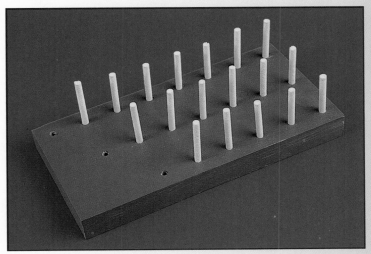

5 Sand dowels and board. Finish with shellac or linseed oil or paint, if desired.

Rules and Strategy

1 Players alternately remove one or more pegs at each turn, but pegs must be taken from one row only. (One or more pegs may be taken even though there are spaces in the row.)
2 The player forced to take the last peg loses.
3 In a series of games, players must alternate going first or second.

Challenge

Does the first or second player have the advantage in this game?

Find two opening moves that will give the second player the advantage.

Find two opening moves that will give the first player the advantage.

Hints   Take care not to make equal rows when taking from any group of three rows. If after taking, you leave 5 − 5 − 3, 4 − 4 − 2, 3 − 3 − 4, or other similar arrangements, you run the risk that your opponent will take all of the uneven group leaving 5 − 5, 4 − 4, 3 − 3, or 2 − 2—all losing positions.

On the other hand, if your opponent leaves you with 5 − 5 − 3, 4 − 4 − 2, 3 − 3 − 4, or 2 − 2 − 3, you would take the uneven group and leave him with 5 − 5, 4 − 4, 3 − 3, or 2 − 2—all losing positions for him. (See solutions at left.)

Solutions to Petals Around the Rose

Challenge 1 The only significant dice in solving this puzzle are the 3 and 5 dice. The 3 die has a single spot (rose) surrounded by two other spots. Therefore, the 3 die is considered to have "two petals around the rose."

Similarly, the 5 die has a single spot (rose) surrounded by four other spots. Then the 5 die has "four petals around the rose."

Examine the first roll on page 69.

The dice in order are: 3, 4, 1, 6, 5.

Ignoring the 4, 1, and 6 dice, one can easily see that the 3 die has two spots (petals) around the central spot. The 5 die also has four spots around the central spot. Therefore, the answer to this roll of the dice is 2 + 4 = 6.

The third roll on that same page has the dice in this order: 3, 3, 3, 6, 5.
Again, ignore the 6. Each 3 has two petals around the rose. Three 2s = 3 x 2 = 6.
The 5 has four petals. The answer to this roll, therefore, is 6 + 4 = 10.

Challenge 2 Similar to the first solution, now consider each die to be a transparent block of ice. The values assigned are the same as in the first challenge: 2 for the 3 die and 4 for the 5 die. The 2 and the 4 are assumed to be seals that come out of the center hole.

The difference in this challenge is that instead of reading the top or face values of the dice, you read the spots on the bottom or underside of each die. Therefore the significant dice are the 2, whose underside is 5, and the 4, whose underside is 3. Answer to top row is 4 + 2 = 6. The 5 as in the petals represents 4; the 3 represents 2.

68

Solution to *How to Weigh a Human Hair*

There are two steps to determine the weight of the paper weights used on the scale.

	Standard USA Measure—(lbs. and oz)		Standard Metric Measure—(kg and g)	
1)	$\dfrac{\text{weight of a ream of paper in lbs}}{500}$ = weight of 1 sheet in lbs.		$\dfrac{\text{weight of a ream of paper in kg}}{500}$ = weight of 1 sheet in kg
2)	weight of 1 sheet (above) X 16 = weight of 1 sheet in oz.		weight of 1 sheet (above) X 1000 = weight of 1 sheet in g

If the paper weights are in square centimeters, then the weight of one sheet must be divided by the number of square centimeters in one sheet. Since one sheet measures 28 cm x 21.5 cm, its area is 602 square centimeters. Therefore, the weight of one square centimeter of paper equals the weight obtained in (2) above divided by 602.

If the paper weights are in ½-in squares, then the weight of one sheet must first be divided by the number of square inches in one sheet. Since a standard sheet is 8½ in x 11 in, that number is 93.5 square inches. Therefore, the weight of one square inch of paper equals the weight obtained in (2) above divided by 93.5.

But since there are four ½-in squares in each square inch of paper, the weight of one square inch of paper obtained by dividing by 93.5 must be divided again by 4. Another way is to divide the weight obtained in (2) by 374. We use 374 because there are 374 ½-in squares in one sheet of paper.

Petals Around the Rose

This game is quite simple yet it creates a challenge that few can resist. The challenge, of course, is to discover the secret that gives the answer for any roll of five dice. For example, the answer to the faces of the dice in the photograph is six.

Materials Needed
Strip of wood 5 in (12.7 cm) by 1 in x 1 in (2.5 cm x 2.5 cm) cross section
Saw
Sandpaper
Felt marker

Construction

1 Cut five 1-in (2.5-cm) cubes. Sand surfaces and edges.

2 Using the felt marker, put dots to correspond to a regular die. Be sure that opposite sides of each die add to seven. (Opposite sides are 1 and 6, 2 and 5, and 3 and 4.)

Challenge 1

The object is to discover the secret of the Petals Around the Rose. In other words, you must find the key that gives the answer for any roll of five dice on the basis of only these three clues:
1 The name of the game is Petals Around the Rose and the name is important.
2 The answer for any roll is always even.
3 When the secret is known, you can tell the single answer for any particular roll of the dice.

Challenge 2

This game is somewhat related to the "Petals" secret. However, this challenge has an unusually long name, "Seals That Come Out of the Hole in the Ice." The information hints for this "secret" are the same as those for the "Petals" problem. Study the title with a creative mind, and see if you can figure out why there are six, four, or fourteen "seals that come out of the ice."
(See solutions on page 68.)

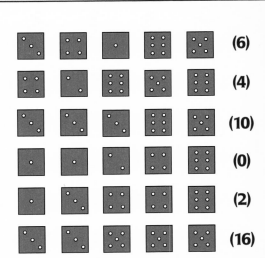

Here are some typical rolls with answer printed at the side.

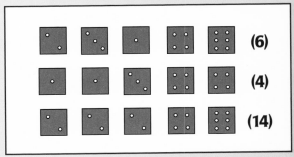

69

Real Life Experiments in Math

How to Weigh a Human Hair

Do you believe that you can weigh a human hair with a scale you can make by yourself in a few minutes? Believe it or not, you really can! Make the scale by using a straw as a lever, a matchbox as a fulcrum, and small centimeter-size squares as weights. With a little arithmetic and a little science, you can perform this experiment as accurately as if you were using an expensive laboratory scale. Dr. Jerrold R. Zacharias and his Science Committee use math and common household materials to do things as well as complex devices do.

Materials Needed
2 matchbook covers
Needle
2 soda straws
Aluminum foil
Sheet of square centimeter paper
Sheet of square inch paper
Razor
3 strands of human hair

Sharp materials are used in this project. Younger children should ask an adult for help.

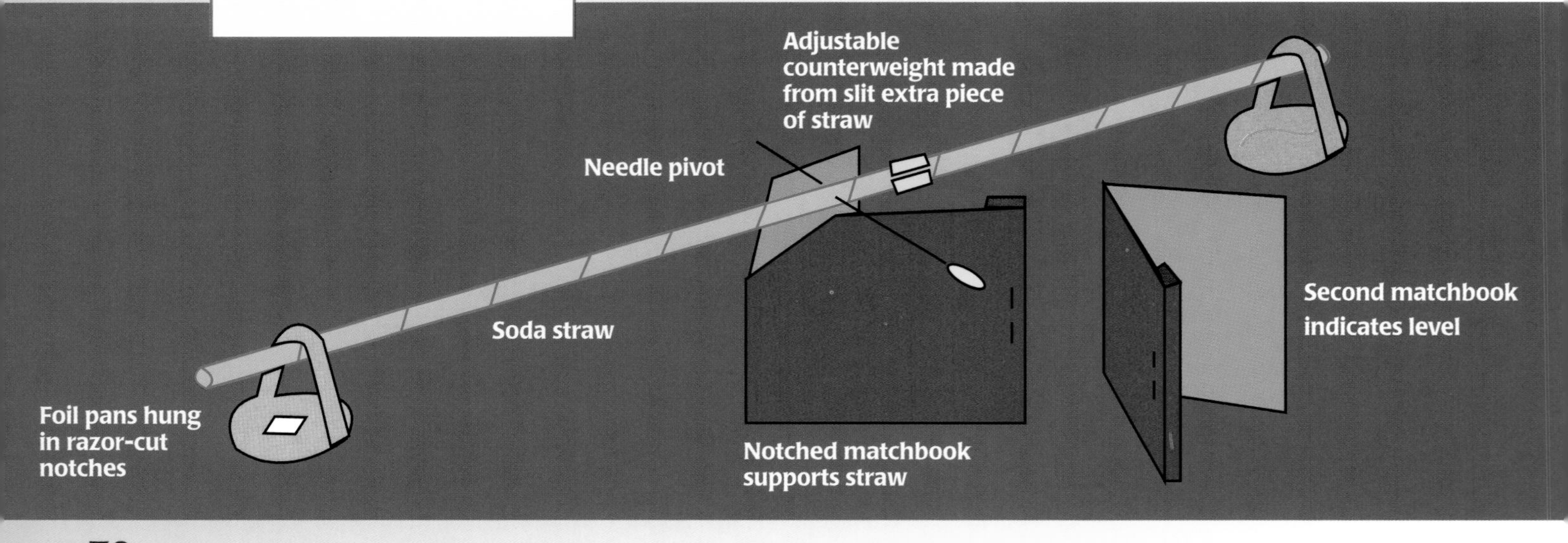

Adjustable counterweight made from slit extra piece of straw

Needle pivot

Second matchbook indicates level

Soda straw

Foil pans hung in razor-cut notches

Notched matchbook supports straw

Construction

1 Puncture the soda straw at the center with a needle. (See diagram page 70.)

2 Notch one matchbook cover and lay the straw on its two edges

3 Shape two identical foil baskets from aluminum foil, then place them on opposite ends of the straw. Each basket should weigh the same amount for the scale to work properly.

4 Cut a ½ in (1.3 cm) piece of straw from the second straw. Slit it and slide it on the whole straw to balance the scale. (See diagram page 70.)

5 Use the second matchbook cover to act as a level.

6 Using the squares at right as a guide, make several paper "weights" for determining the weight of a human hair.

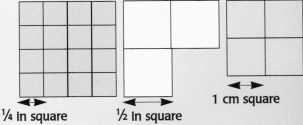

¼ in square   ½ in square   1 cm square

Challenge

How do you determine the weight of the paper weights to use?

Hint Divide the weight of one ream of sheets by the number of sheets in a ream to get the weight of one sheet. (Divide by 500.)

Using centimeter-ruled paper, compare the weight of a carefully cut piece with the area of the whole sheet. The piece can be a 2-cm square, a 4-cm square, an 8-cm square, or a 10-cm square piece.

Your answer will be a fraction $\dfrac{2}{\text{sq cm in 1 sheet}}$, $\dfrac{4}{\text{sq cm in 1 sheet}}$, $\dfrac{8}{\text{sq cm in 1 sheet}}$, or $\dfrac{10}{\text{sq cm in 1 sheet}}$

This fraction will be the fraction that you multiply by the weight of one sheet. (The weight you arrived at from step 1 when you divided the ream weight by 500.)

Experiment

Place the human hair on one of the foil pans. Using paper squares of 2, 4, 8, or 10 square centimeter sizes, determine the weight of two or three different strands of hair.

Using paper squares of ¼ square inch, ½ square in, and 1 square in sizes, weigh strands again.

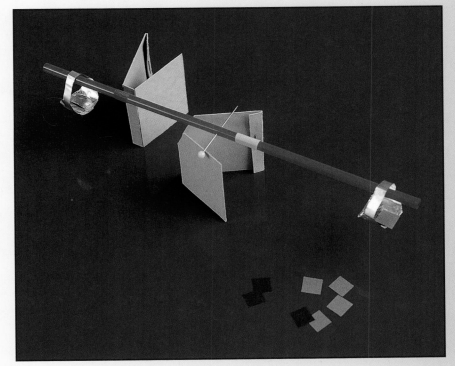

Compare the results of weighing with centimeter squares and with inch squares.
Which seems to be more accurate? (See solution on page 68.)

One-Sided Strips and Other Surprises

A mathematician confided
That a Möbius is one-sided,
And you'll get quite a laugh
If you cut one in half.
For it stays in one piece when divided!

This poem tells of only one magical thing about a Möbius strip. After doing more experiments with Möbius strips and other paper bands, you'll be amazed at the results.

Materials Needed

Paper strips 2 in (5.1 cm) wide (or adding machine paper roll)
Paper strips 3 in (7.6 cm) wide
Scissors
Tape or stapler
Red and green colored pencils

Construction

1 Cut four strips of paper and mark corners, as shown.

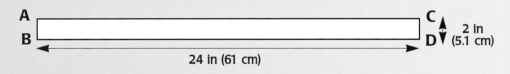

A

B

C

D

2 in (5.1 cm)

24 in (61 cm)

2 Join the ends of each as shown and described below:

Notice the first construction (Strip 1). It is a simple band, like an ordinary belt with two faces: one inside and one outside face. This is

Strip 1 Make a simple band by attaching the ends together with tape. Join **A** to **C** and **B** to **D**.

Strip 2 Give strip a half twist. Join **A** to **D**, **B** to **C**.

Strip 3 Give strip two half twists. Join **A** to **C**, and **B** to **D**.

Strip 4 Give strip three half twists. Join **A** to **D**, and **B** to **C**.

not a Möbius strip but a common ring or paper belt. In 1858, a German mathematician, August Ferdinand Möbius, discovered that if you give a band a half twist, and then attach the ends together, it becomes an interesting plaything with unusual characteristics.

Experiment 1   Using the second strip, imagine the strip to be a road. Using two colored pencils, red and green, start drawing a red center line with the red pencil along the top of the strip. Directly underneath the red line start drawing with the green color as far as you can. What happens will contradict everything we have learned about the top and bottom of a belt or ring of paper. The red and green lines will, unbelievably, meet! It proves that there is no top or bottom to this strip. It is really a one-sided piece of paper!

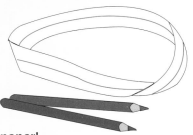

Experiment 2   There is a story of a Persian ruler who posed this problem to select a smart husband for his daughter. The daughter would take the hand of the man who could connect the pairs of like numbers with lines that must not cross any other lines. Draw on a strip of paper the numbers, 1, 2, 3, as shown.
How would you solve this problem?

1 2 3		3 2 1

Experiment 3

Take the Möbius strip used in experiment 1. Cut along the center line you have drawn all around the strip. Now you should know one secret magicians use to fool you. What happens?

With another similar band, cut all around it again, keeping your scissors about one-third the distance from the edge at all times. What happens?

Try twisting and cutting several other bands using the suggestions at right. How many sides and edges are created? How many twists and loops? (See solutions on page 74.)

Number of half twists	Kind of cut
0	center
1	center
1	one-third
2	center
2	one-third
3	center
3	one-third

Experiment 4   Construct a double Möbius strip by placing two strips together, one on top of the other. Then, holding them apart with a finger in between them at both ends, give them both a half twist. Tape the ends together and hang them from a support or string. If stiff paper is used it will appear to be two separate bands. While hanging, place a pencil in between the strips and run it all the way around the bands, returning to the place you had started. In a similar manner, a bug could crawl between the bands and go round and round forever, as if it were walking between two surfaces where one was the ceiling and the other was the floor.

Problem   Are there really two separate bands? Hold one piece and shake it.
              Amazing! One single band! Why?

Experiment 5   Place two strips, one 2 in (5.1 cm) wide and one 3 in (7.6 cm) wide, at right angles. Staple in the position of a cross, as shown. Bring the top edge to the bottom edge and attach with tape; then bring the right edge to the left edge of the second strip and attach to form a circular loop. When completed, you will have two circular loops at right angles to each other. Cut down the center of each loop, one at a time. Try to visualize the result. Then make the two cuts and note the surprising shape you have formed. If you have guessed the shape beforehand, you are one person in a hundred! Try this magic on your friends.

73

Solutions to One-Sided Strips and Other Surprises

Experiment 1 The green line (apparently on the top) will soon meet the red line which had been started (presumably underneath) on the bottom. The contradiction occurs because the strip, when given a half twist, becomes a Möbius strip which has only one side; therefore, the red and green lines must meet.

Experiment 2 The solution to the Persian ruler's problem is found by giving the strip a half twist after labeling one end 1, 2, 3 and the opposite end 3, 2, 1. Lines connecting the like numbers without crossing are now a simple matter.

Experiment 3 The secret that magicians often use is to cut a Möbius strip completely along its center. The surprising result is that only one band remains although the strip has been cut in half. When the band is again cut around, but not in the center and one third the distance from the edge, another surprise occurs. Two interlocking rings are formed.

Experiment 4 The amazing result that occurs when a double Möbius strip is taken apart demonstrates that it is actually a single band. Although there were two bands originally before being twisted and joined, even with your fingers between the bands, because of the twist, you taped the top and bottom together to form a single band!

Experiment 5 Since the two strips were taped or stapled at right angles before being joined into two loops, when the two loops were cut in half, a perfect square was formed. The four right angles that were originally present before cutting simply became inverted to form the four inner corners of the resulting square.

Experiment 6 As in experiment 5, the two strips were also joined at right angles. The only difference was that one strip was longer than the other. Therefore, when cut, a rectangle was formed because two of the opposite sides were longer as a result of the longer strips. Four right angles were again formed because they were originally joined at right angles.

Experiment 7 Since the two strips in this experiment were attached to form an X, they obviously did not form right angles. Consequently, when the two loops were cut, neither square nor rectangle occurred. A rhombus was formed. However, if the strips were not the same length, the more common parallelogram would have resulted.

MÖBIUS STRIP FACT SHEET

Number of half twists	Number of sides and edges	Kind of cut	Result of cut: Number of sides & edges Number of twists & loops
0	2 sides, 2 edges	center	2 loops, each with 2 sides and 2 edges
1	1 side, 2 edges	center	1 loop, twice the length, 2 twists
1	1 side, 2 edges	one-third	2 loops, 1 half twist, and 1 full twist
2	2 sides, 2 edges	center	2 loops, each with 2 sides and 2 edges; each with 2 half twists
2	2 sides, 2 edges	one-third	2 loops, each with 2 sides and 2 edges; 1 loop twice as wide as other loop
3	1 side, 2 edges	center	2 loops, each with one side, 3 twists
3	1 side, 2 edges	one-third	2 loops, each with 1 side, 3 twists, one twice as long as the other

Experiment 6

Place two other strips at right angles as in experiment 5, and perform the same cutting operations except for one thing. These two strips are not the

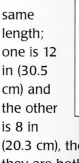

same length; one is 12 in (30.5 cm) and the other is 8 in (20.3 cm), though they are both 3 in (7.6 cm) wide. After experiment 5, this shape should be quite easy to visualize.

Experiment 7

Now place two other strips at angles to form an "X." Attach opposite ends together

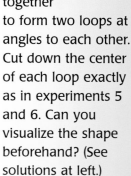

to form two loops at angles to each other. Cut down the center of each loop exactly as in experiments 5 and 6. Can you visualize the shape beforehand? (See solutions at left.)

Form Any Shape on This Geoboard and Find Its Area by Magic

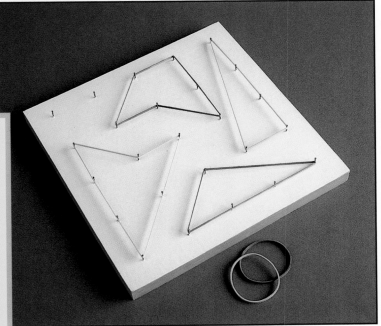

With this common grid of nails, you can do more than form many geometric shapes and symmetrical designs. You can perform the spectacular feat of finding the area of regular or jagged intricate shapes using the magical formula learned in this activity. With this secret formula you can actually do what appears to be impossible. Have a friend make the most complicated shape on the board with a rubber band. You can relay how large it is in less than a minute!

Materials Needed

Geoboard pattern
Piece of wood 10 in x 10 in (25 cm x 25 cm)
   by ¾ in (1.9 cm) thick
Brads or small nails
Linseed oil, shellac, or paint, if desired
Rubber bands

Construction

1 Photocopy the pattern at right and place it on top of the square board.

2 Tape the corners of the sheet onto the board to keep it in place.

3 Nail the brads or nails on the dots into the board so that each protrudes ½ in (1.3 cm) above the surface. Remove the paper.

4 Sand the board and finish with shellac, oil, or paint. Dry completely.

Activity

Connect nails with rubber bands and design the maximum area for the polygons listed below:

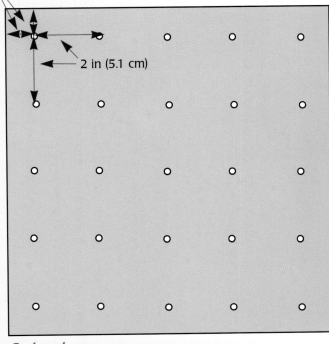

1 in (2.5 cm)

2 in (5.1 cm)

Geoboard pattern

Photocopy geoboard pattern. Enlarge 300%.

Solutions to Form Any Shape on This Geoboard and Find Its Area by Magic

Easier exercises

parallelogram 12 square units
trapezoid 14 square units
rhombus 16 square units

Harder exercises

pentagon 15½ square units
hexagon 15½ square units
octagon 15 square units
decagon 15 square units

Table

b – 8 outside nails	1 inside nail	Area: 4
c – 6 outside nails	2 inside nails	Area: 4
d – 4 outside nails	3 inside nails	Area: 4

Notice all four polygons have the same area – 4 square units!

Solutions to Traveling Paths and Networks

Problem 1 Looking at the seven bridge drawing as Euler simplified and designed it (page 79), you will find odd-numbered vertices at points A, B, C, and D. Three lines meet at points A, B, and D, and five lines meet at point C. The results show that when there are more than two odd-numbered vertices on a network, the path cannot be traveled without retracing some of your steps.

Problem 2 If you built a bridge from point A to point C, both of these vertices would become even numbered (four lines meeting at point A and six lines meeting at point C). Since there would be only two odd-numbered vertices at B and D, the road then could be traveled without retracing.

If you demolished one of the bridges, the one from C to D, the new network would then have four lines meeting at C, and two lines at D, making them both even vertices. Since that would leave only odd vertices at A and B, the path could be traveled without retracing.

> **Euler's Rule** When there are more than two odd-numbered vertices, the path cannot be traveled without retracing some of the lines.

Network	Number of odd vertices	Number of even vertices	Can it be traveled?
C	2	2	yes
D	2	4	yes
E	4	4	no
F	0	10	yes
G	0	12	yes
H	0	16	yes
I	2	2	yes
J	2	3	yes

Easier exercises

square — 16 square units
rectangle — 12 square units
triangle — 8 square units

What are the maximum areas for: Parallelogram, trapezoid, rhombus.

Harder exercises These polygons have maximum areas greater than fourteen square units.

Design the shape and find the area for each. Pentagon, hexagon, octagon, decagon. (See solutions at left.)

Activity

With a rubber band, construct polygons **a**, **b**, **c**, and **d**, as shown. Figure the area for each. The area for **a** is shown on page 77. (See solutions for **b**, **c**, and **d** at left.)

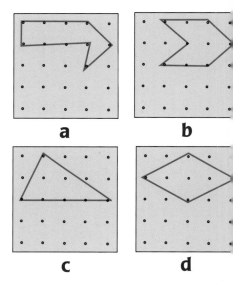

a

b

c

d

• What do you notice about the areas of the four polygons?

• What do you see happening to the number of outside nails? (The ones touching the rubber band on the four polygons.)

• What do you notice about the

Figure	Outside nails	Inside nails	Subtract	Area
a	10	0	1	4

number of inside nails? (The nails within the four polygons, not touching the band.)

Examine the four squares that can be constructed with a rubber band on this geoboard. In each of these squares the dot represents a nail. Count the number of outside nails (those touching the boundary line) in each square. Then count the number of inside nails (those not touching the outside line).

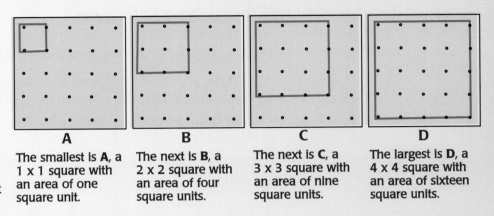

A	B	C	D
The smallest is **A**, a 1 x 1 square with an area of one square unit.	The next is **B**, a 2 x 2 square with an area of four square units.	The next is **C**, a 3 x 3 square with an area of nine square units.	The largest is **D**, a 4 x 4 square with an area of sixteen square units.

The table below will help you count the number of outside and inside nails for each square. Now notice the remarkable coincidence between all the areas of the four squares and all the sums of ½ outside nails + inside nails:

	Table on the left (outside + inside)		Table on the right (outside + inside)				
Square	Outside nails	Inside nails	½ outside nails	+	inside nails	=	sum
A	4	0	2	+	0	=	2
B	8	1	4	+	1	=	5
C	12	4	6	+	4	=	10
D	16	9	8	+	9	=	17

Square **A** — Area (1x1) = 1 square unit, sum of ½ outside + inside = 2
Square **B** — Area (2x2) = 4 square units, sum of ½ outside + inside = 5
Square **C** — Area (3x3) = 9 square units, sum of ½ outside + inside = 10
Square **D** — Area (4x4) = 16 square units, sum of ½ outside + inside = 17

The areas of all the squares is always one less than ½ outside + inside nails! (1 is one less than 2; 4 is one less than 5; 9 is one less than 10; and 16 is one less than 17!)

The unique relationship governing areas and the number of outside and inside nails can be stated as follows: The area of each of these squares is always one less than the sum of half of the outside nails plus the inside nails.

Pick's Area Formula

(for finding any area bounded by a rubber band on a geoboard)

$$A = \frac{1}{2}(O) + I - 1$$

A (area), **O** (boundary or outside nails), and **I** (inside nails)

This amazing formula can give you the area of any shape of geometric figure on any size grid of nails with any length rubber band. To have fun and amaze your friends, hand them a rubber band, tell them to form the most intricate or jagged figure they can produce. In a moment, you immediately announce the area using Pick's (named for the discoverer, Georg Pick) formula. (See solutions on page 76.)

Traveling Paths and Networks

A river runs through the city of Königsberg and the land is interconnected by seven bridges, as shown. What is the quickest way to stroll around the city, crossing every bridge only once? Leonhard Euler of Switzerland solved the problem, can you?

To solve the problem, people try to draw figures without retracing the same line twice. Drawings A through J below are some good examples of "trips" to take around a figure without retracing lines. Some of these trips can be done without retracing steps but others cannot be done the quickest way. Take your time in drawing the figures and notice why some can be drawn without retracing and others cannot.

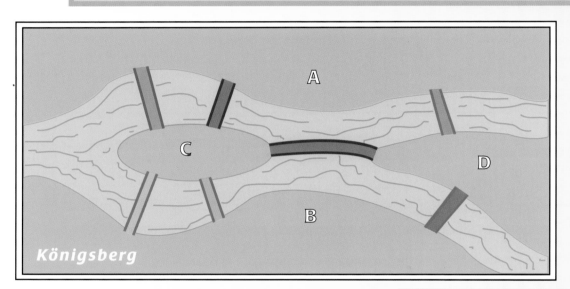

Königsberg

Materials Needed
Sheet of light cardboard
1 sheet each of blue and
    green colored paper
7 colored strips of paper
Scissors
Felt marker
Paste or glue

Construction
1 Simulate the map by cutting out shapes from blue paper to represent the Preger River and pasting them on light cardboard.

2 Then cut green paper to represent the mainland on opposite sides of the river and the two islands, and paste on the cardboard.

3 Paste colored strips as located to represent the famous seven bridges of Königsberg.

Exercise
Can you travel these networks? Photocopy figures **A** through **J** at right. Examine all corners and intersections to see how many lines lead to each point. If there is an odd number of lines (roads)

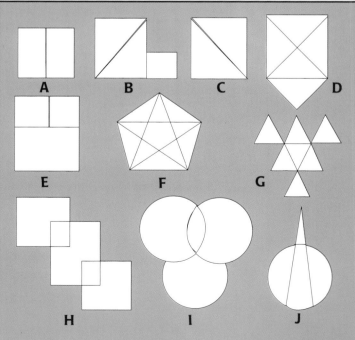

leading to each point, it is an odd vertex. If an even number of roads lead to a point, it's an even vertex, as shown in the figures at below.

Odd vertex

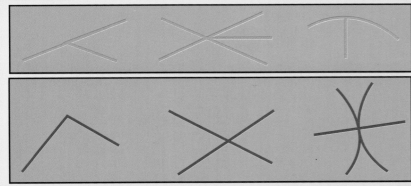

Even vertex

For each of the figures **C** through **J**, count the number of odd vertices and the number of even vertices, as shown for **A** and **B** at left. Decide if the networks can be traveled. After completing and studying the results, can you discover Euler's rule: the number of odd vertices that makes it impossible to travel any network?

Network	Number of odd vertices	Number of even vertices	Can it be traveled?
A	2	4	Yes
B	4	2	No

Acknowledgments

A special thanks to my daughter and her husband, Maria Rowe and Barry Rowe, and Mary Bernhard Lalama for their many hours spent on the text and graphics of the initial stages of this book. I am also particularly indebted to daughter and son-in-law, Dianna and Ivan Strom, for reviewing and editing the final copy, and my grandson, Eric Strom, for creating many of the final graphics.

I must also gratefully acknowledge the following people whose ideas I shared or revised for some of the ideas and activities in this book: Alice Joyce Davidson, James T. Anderson, George Sincherman, Gustavas Simmons, Kurt Christoff, Dr. Jerrold R. Zacharias, Clifford Adams, the railroad clerk who discovered the only magic hexagon, and Georg Pick, the Czechoslovakian mathematician who discovered Pick's Theorem, and to my son, Angelo Lobosco, who invented the original mind reading activity with triangle cards.

EULER'S SIMPLIFIED DRAWING OF THE PROBLEM

A—Land area north of river

C

D— island

B—Land area south of river

Problem 1
The famous network of the seven bridges is condensed at left, as Euler brilliantly simplified and designed. Take the original drawing of the river and bridges of this activity shown on page 78. Imagine the land areas on both sides of the river shrinking to points **A** and **B**, and the islands in the river shrinking to points **C** and **D**. Consider the six arcs and the straight line to be the seven bridges; and the stroll around the city will look like the network at left.

Using what you have discovered, can you or can you not travel the seven bridges just once?

Problem 2
Could you help the people of Königsberg take a similar stroll by building another bridge? Could you solve the problem another way by demolishing one of the bridges? If so, which one would you destroy? (See solutions on page 76.)

Index